The Butterfly Bride

Previously published books by
T. Mike Walker:

Voices From the Bottom of the World: A Policeman's Journal, Grove
Press, 1970 fiction. 286 pgs Available from www.Amazon.com

RESPECT, Town Scribe Publications & Global Books, 2003,
fiction 467 pgs Available on-line from www.booksurge.com

The Butterfly Bride and other Tales of a Traveling Minister, Town
Scribe Publications & Global Books, 2004. Non-fiction 145 pgs
Available online from www.booksurge.com

Special Credits:

Bridal Trends Magazine, 1994, *"The Wedding Kiss"*

Good Times, Santa Cruz weekly entertainment guide,
published early versions of many of the essays and tales
collected here.

Kurtz Photographics
3980-A Research Park Court, Soquel, CA 95073
Telephone [831] 465-9700 Facsimile [831] 465-9705
Email: steve@kurtzphoto.com

Illuminations by Sandra

Paul Meglson Photographer, 831-207-9145

Terry Way (photo); phone: (831) 464-0939, info@terryway.com

Cover design by Ron Septimus, www.SantaCruzDSL.com

The Butterfly Bride
And Other Tales of a Traveling Minister

T. Mike Walker

Town Scribe Books
2004

Published by **Town Scribe Books**
www.townscribe.com
Santa Cruz, CA. 95060
Order from www.booksurge.com

Printed by **Global Books**,
270 King Street
Charleston, SC 29401

To order additional copies, please contact us.
BookSurge, LLC
www.booksurge.com
1-866-308-6235
orders@booksurge.com

The Butterfly Bride

Chapter Index

This book is dedicated to the hundreds of couples who, over the past thirty years, placed their trust in me by choosing me to be their wedding minister. Thank you so much! I have gathered a bouquet of your beautiful love stories here, culled from a few of my favorite weddings. My hope is that your stories will inspire others to create their own unique wedding ceremony for their own special day.

Special thanks and heartfelt hugs to my wife, *Sandra Vines-Walker*—your loving support, illuminations, and suggestions for this book have been invaluable.

I offer praise and appreciation to *Allison, Aurora, Dusty, Donita, Elizabeth, Janeen, Margy, Mary Lou*, and *Shannon*, ten wonderful wedding coordinators who have served as mentors and models to me over the years.

***

Some names have been changed to protect the privacy of individuals.

Part One: The Butterfly Bride

"Love indeed is light from heaven,
A spark of that immortal life."
Lord Byron

The Butterfly Bride

Perched on a hill looking over Santa Cruz and the sparkling Monterey bay, Chaminade Resort and Spa was originally a Catholic seminary and retreat center. About twenty years ago it was sold to a business group who transformed the old buildings into an elegant, First Class resort. Weddings occur there on a regular basis, but the wedding coordinator confessed to me after one ceremony I performed there a few years ago that she'd never seen anything quite like it.

Neither had I.

The Element of Surprise

Gwen was a slender blonde with fine, delicate features. Doug was only a few inches taller, wearing large rimless glasses and a boyish smile. "We want our wedding to be full of surprises. Think you can handle that?"

"I love surprises," I confessed. "Providing they aren't too surprising...."

They both laughed, squeezing each others hands. "We also want to write our own vows," Gwen insisted.

"We've got friends who want to do special readings during the ceremony," Doug added.

"And we're going to release butterflies at the end," Gwen said, her hands fluttering upward over her head.

"Why butterflies? What do they symbolize to you?"

She looked puzzled. "I don't know. I just thought they'd be beautiful."

"They will be," I agreed. "But I could also say something about their special meaning to your guests. For instance, for some people butterflies symbolize transformation."

"That sounds good, but we'll have to get back to you on that," Doug said.

"I'm curious—where are you getting the butterflies, and how are they going to arrive at Chaminade—via Air Mail?"

"They *will* be in envelopes," Gwen laughed.

"But we're not going to mail them," Doug assured me. "My brother will pick them up the morning of our wedding at a place called *Magical Beginnings* in Los Altos. It's a butterfly farm."

Doug explained that the insects would be kept dormant in special, unsealed envelopes until their release at the end of the ceremony.

We talked for over an hour. The challenge was to keep everything fresh from beginning to end. Then I set to work transforming their ideas into the first draft of their ceremony.

The Ceremony

On the day of the wedding, the usual summer fog cleared just in time for the guests to be seated in the welcoming sun.

As they followed me down the aisle, the Groom, Best Man and Groomsmen, all dressed in tuxedoes, passed out the special envelopes to pre-selected people at the end of each row of chairs, and then took their places beside me at the wedding arch.

The photographers were positioned with their cameras and video equipment ready. I nodded to the wedding coordinator to let her know we were in place. The flute and guitar duo off to the side of the wedding arch took their cue and struck up the strains of Pachelbelle's Cannon in D.

Four Bridesmaids and the Maid of Honor started down the aisle, single file. They wore matching soft blue satin dresses that accented their beauty. They took their places at the wedding arch and I said, *"Please rise for the entrance of the Bride!"*

The musicians struck up the wedding march as Gwen entered with her Father.

They stopped at the first row of seats and I asked, *"Who brings this woman to be wed?"*

"Her mother and I do, with our blessings," Gwen's father said. He lifted her veil and kissed her. Their eyes were glistening with tears of joy.

Doug stepped forward and shook his hand, then escorted Gwen back to the wedding arch where they stood facing each other in front of me.

I asked the guests to be seated, and then welcomed them to the wedding of Doug and Gwen. I also welcomed those who could not be with us in body, but who were with us in Spirit. I thanked them for driving all those extra miles so Doug and Gwen could hold their wedding outdoors in this beautiful location, overlooking the Bay, and I reminded them how important they were to Gwen and Doug as their supporting community.

Next I said, *"Today Gwen and Doug marry each other, but they also join each other's families as well. Two long lines of ancestors converge in them to bring forth the future. Therefore I would say to the parents of Gwen and Doug that if you will accept your new son in law as your son and accept our new daughter in law as your daughter, they can begin their lives together as a married couple standing on the solid foundation of your love and support. You were their first models of love, and the values you gave them have helped shape them into the beautiful young people who stand before us today. They would like to take this moment to thank you for all your hard work and support. As a special way of saying thanks to all of you at once, Gwen and Doug would like to give gifts of flowers to their mothers and grandmothers."*

Gwen handed her bouquet to her Maid of Honor as the musicians played a sweet improvisation in the background. Gwen and Doug untied flowers from the arch; they went together first to Gwen's mother and grandmothers, then to Doug's mother and grandmothers, gifting them with flowers. They also gave hugs and kisses to their dads.

That was their first surprise.

They returned to their positions, holding hands as they faced each other in front of me. I said, *"Next, Gwen and Doug have asked Doug's Uncle Bill to read "I do not love you,' by the late great Spanish poet, Pablo Neruda."*

Uncle Bill stepped forward to the microphone. His voice was sweet and warm, filled with compassion as he read:

"I do not love you as if you were salt-rose, or topaz,
Or the arrow of carnations the fire shoots off.
I love you as certain dark things are to be loved,
In secret, between the shadow and the soul.
I love you as the plant that never blooms
But carries in itself the light of hidden flowers;
Thanks to your love a certain solid fragrance,
Risen from the earth, lives darkly in my body
I love you without knowing how, or when, or from where.
I love you straightforwardly, without complexities or pride;
So I love you because I know no other way
Than this: where I does not exist, nor you,
So close that your hand on my chest is my hand,
So close that your eyes close as I fall asleep."

Uncle Bill returned to his seat and I continued, *"Gwen and Doug have asked Gwen's Aunt Rose to sing 'Give Yourself to Love,' by Kate Wolfe."*

Rose approached the microphone from the other side of the aisle as the music duet struck up the song. Rose was a professional singer, and she understood the lyrics well. She sang them with deep warmth of feeling and had all the guests singing the chorus with her at the end.

"Give Yourself To Love"

Kind friends all gather round to celebrate the way
That which brings us together here has blessed us all today
Love has made a circle that holds us all inside
Where strangers are as family and loneliness can't hide...

> **Chorus:** *You must give yourself to love*
> *Love is what you're after*
> *Open up your hearts to*
> *The tears and the laughter*
> *And give yourself to love*
> *Give yourself to love*

I've walked these mountains in the rain,
I've learned to love the wind
I've been up before the sunrise to watch the day begin
I always knew I'd find you though I never did know how
But like sunshine on a cloudy day you stand before me now

> **Chorus:** *So I give myself to love*
> *Love is what I'm after*
> *I open up my heart to*
> *The tears and the laughter*
> *And give myself to love*
> *I give myself to love*

Love is born in fire, just like the Redwood seed
And love can't give me everything but it gives me what I need
Love came to me not ready. It came when I was afraid
It will be my greatest teacher. You're the best friend I have made.

> **Chorus:** *So I give myself to love, etc...*

When she finished, we were all in tears.

Their Love Story

The next surprise was their story. I continued, "*Thank you, Aunt Rose, for your beautiful gift of that song. Love is definitely what we're after here today. As some of you may know, Gwen and Doug believe that Fate had a hand in bringing them together. They met in 1993 at UCSC when they lived next door to each other in the dorms. Over the next few months of their developing relationship they learned that they both grew up in San Jose, where they lived just minutes from each other's homes. They had attended the same junior high and high schools without ever meeting. Their opening conversations quickly led them into friendship and they soon became inseparable. Gwen fell in love with Doug's spirit of adventure, his spontaneity, and his sense of humor. Doug was drawn to Gwen's kindness, quick wit, and loving nature. They enjoyed driving up and down the coast, exploring the beaches from Half Moon Bay to Big Sur. They especially loved the hot tubs at Esselin, where they went for midnight soaks after exams. Doug proposed to Gwen on the beach in Carmel at sunset. He brought a picnic basket complete with two tulips—her favorite flower—and a bottle of champagne with one glass. When he knelt down in the sand, Gwen said, 'What are you doing?'*

"*'Proposing to you, of course. Now stop a minute and answer my question—will you share the cup of life with me, and be my wife?'*

"*'I thought you'd never ask me! My father told me a month ago that you asked him for permission.' She kissed Doug, smiled, and said, 'The answer is yes.'*

Doug uncorked the bottle and they toasted their future. He also offered Gwen a chocolate ring, since he hadn't had a chance to buy her a real one yet. Gwen graciously accepted the ring, slipped it onto her finger—then proceeded to eat it!

Don't worry—Doug assured me that today's rings are made of sterner stuff.

May we have the real rings for presentation?"

Rings and Vows

The Best man removed the rings from their boxes and placed them in my palm. I said, "*Your rings are round, like the earth and the moon that circle each other like husband and wife. They will serve as reminders to you and to others of the promises you make here today, and you may exchange them as you speak your vows.*

"Doug, please take Gwen's ring and repeat after me: Gwen, today I marry you, my best friend...the one I laugh with...the one I dream with...the one I love... Just as there will never be a morning without the ocean's flow...so there will never be a day without my love for you... I promise to be your devoted husband...dependable as the tide; just as water nourishes the earth and sustains life...may my constant love nourish and sustain you... With this ring I marry you...and pledge my faithful love."

He placed the ring on her finger.

Gwen took Doug's ring and repeated after me: *"Doug, today I marry you, my best friend...the one I laugh with...the one I dream with...the one I love......may our love always be as constant and unchanging...Just as the never-ending ocean waves...flow endlessly from the depths of the sea...I promise to be your devoted wife...As bounded to you as the tide is to the moon...With this ring I marry you...and pledge my faithful love."*

She placed the ring on his finger.

Pronouncement of Marriage

I said, *"Your two lives are now joined in one unbroken circle. We pray that you find in each other the lasting love for which all men and women yearn. Doug and Gwen, you have consented together to marriage before your family and friends; you have pledged your faith and declared your unity by giving and receiving rings as seals of your esteem and devotion. Therefore, as a Minister of the Universal Life Church and in accord with the laws of the State of California, I pronounce that you are husband and wife. Please seal your marriage with a kiss."*

They kissed and the guests applauded.

Butterfly Release

Finally, I said, *"All over the world Butterflies symbolize transformation. Even though Butterflies are fragile creatures, many Oriental cultures consider them to symbolize lasting married love. May today's transformation of Doug and Gwen, from two individuals into their life together as husband and wife, endure and prosper!"*

At this cue the pre-determined guests sitting at the ends of the aisles opened their envelopes and three dozen brilliant orange, yellow and black Monarch butterflies flew into the air as I said, *"Ladies and Gentlemen, please stand for the exit of the Bridal Party and welcome Doug and Gwen into your hearts."*

The musicians struck up a bright and bouncy Gaelic tune. Arm in arm, the Bride and Groom skipped up the aisle. Attracted by Gwen's flowing lace veil, the butterflies followed the Bride, circling around her head as she moved across the courtyard. In fact, they trailed her through her wedding pictures, swirling around the patio for over an hour before they flew off down the hill toward a grove of Eucalyptus trees, searching for something to eat and drink, like all the other wedding guests.

The Elopement

Webster's Encyclopedic Unabridged Dictionary of the English Language defines *elope* as "…to run off secretly to be married, usually without the consent or knowledge of one's parents; to run away with a lover; to leave without permission or notification; escape." The word derives from Middle English (1590-1600), *alopen,* to run away.

Evidently, people have been doing it for hundreds of years!

While there might be many good reasons to run, one wedding I performed early in my ministry illustrated both the need for couples to be able to elope, if they so desire, and the need for Officiants who can enable such escapes. Over time, I have come to appreciate the evolution of 24-Hour Drive-Through wedding chapels in places like Reno and Las Vegas.

Eloping is not merely spontaneously running off to get married; often it is a last resort. Seen from one angle, it is a desperate gesture of defiance. From another view, It can be a courageous act of affirmation. No one else can live your life for you, and you're entitled to make your own decisions. So when push comes to shove, if your hearts are united—it's okay to run for your life!

Answering the call

One afternoon about a year after I received my minister's license, I received an unusual phone call. The young man's voice was shaky, almost hesitant at first. "I was given your number by a mutual friend, but I can't reveal his name. How soon could you perform a wedding for my finance and I?"

"How soon do you need it?"

"Could you do it today?"

"Of course. Usually I sit down with each couple and discuss your ceremony first, including the story of how you met, why you chose your wedding site, plus anything else that you want said or read or sung at your ceremony…"

"We won't need all that. Don't you have a short ceremony you can read? It doesn't have to be religious. We just want to say, 'I do.'"

"Sure. I can stitch together something short and sweet. Where and at what time do you want to get married?"

"Could we come to your house in an hour?"

The eagerness in his voice was infectious. "Yes, but you *will* need a marriage license to make it legal," I reminded him.

"We have one. We'll bring it with us."

"You'll also need at least one witness to sign it, as well."

There was a slight pause, and he sighed. "Okay, I'll bring my Best Man. But you have to promise not to tell anyone else that we came to you or reveal our names."

"You have my confidentiality. But listen—I don't want to be involved in anything illegal, either."

"Don't worry; we're not breaking any laws—unless they're in-laws." He laughed at his own joke. "Where do you live?"

I gave him directions to my house and hung up the phone. Then, based on our brief conversation, I typed up a one page ceremony containing only the bare essentials. Then I put on my dark suit, white shirt, and a tie for the occasion.

At the appointed hour there was a knock on my door. Standing on my front porch were three people dressed like they just stepped off a Hollywood movie set.

The handsome young groom looked impeccable in his gray tuxedo with tails. His long blonde hair was pulled back in a pony-tail beneath his grey top hat. He wore matching gray leather shoes and spats and carried a slender grey walking cane. His Best Man wore a matching gray tuxedo with shorter tails. Beautiful cream-colored rose boutonnières were pinned on their lapels. They grinned at me, and I half expected them to break into a Fred Aster style soft-shoe dance.

Standing between them, the Bride looked like a queen. A diamond studded silver tiara crowned her shoulder-length lace veil. Her low-cut satin gown trailed a four-foot train. She carried a bouquet of long-stemmed cream colored roses.

I was baffled by their beauty, yet I felt strangely honored.

"Do you want to hold your ceremony inside or out?"

"Outside would be great," the Groom agreed. "We were originally going to be outside at the..."

The Bride touched his hand and he immediately stopped talking.

"Please, follow me." I led them through my living room, kitchen, and laundry room to the back yard where my luxuriant weeds and far-ranging blackberry vines were in full-bloom. I called it my garden, but it was actually more like a jungle.

The Bride and Groom were nervous, excited, and eager to proceed. They faced each other, gazing into each other's eyes and held hands as I asked the Groom, *"Do you take this Woman to be your lawfully wedded wife, to live together in the holy estate of Matrimony? Will you love her, comfort her, honor, and keep her in sickness and in health; and, forsaking all others, keep only unto her, so long as you both shall live?"*

The young man answered, "Absolutely!"

The Bride answered the same question with an eager, "Yes!"

I asked the Best Man, *"Do you have rings?"* He removed two rings from their boxes and dropped them into my open palm. I don't know how many finely cut diamonds were set in those sleek golden bands, but I doubt if I had ever held so much compressed wealth in one hand before. It seemed strange to me that such enormous value could reside in such tiny, seemingly insignificant stones. Yet wars had been fought and millions of destinies changed over diamonds and gold, which many people still seem to believe are more precious than life itself.

The Bride handed her flower bouquet to the Best Man in order to free her hands.

I said: *"Your rings are symbols of your love for each other and you may exchange them now. Please repeat after me..."*

I turned to each of them in turn and said, *"With this ring I marry you and pledge my faithful love."*

They repeated the phrase and took turns placing the rings on each other's fingers.

Finally I said, *"You have pronounced yourselves husband and wife before God and this witness. Please seal your marriage with a kiss."*

As they were kissing, the Best Man pulled out a pocket sized instamatic camera and snapped a picture of them. Then he slapped me a high five. "Right on! Thanks for making this so easy for them, Pastor. Would you mind standing beside them so I can get a picture of all three of you?"

"Never mind all that, Gary," the Groom said, coming up for air. "At least we're legal now. That's what's important."

"Almost legal," I corrected. "It's not actually *legal* until the Best Man and I sign your license, and even then it's only *technically* legal until the County records and files the document. But don't worry, I'll hand deliver it to the County clerk first thing in the morning."

The Best Man produced a 9x12 manila envelope containing the official license and the Bride and Groom's medical forms inside. This was back during the days when California couples were still required to get blood tests prior to marriage. I filled in the bottom of the license and signed it, then showed the Best Man where to sign to make it official. The Best Man took a picture of me signing the license, and then I took a picture of him doing the same. Finally I took several pictures of the three of them together in front of my wild rose and black berry bushes.

As they were about to leave, I couldn't hold back my curiosity. "You kids were obviously prepared for a major blowout at some expensive location—what happened? Why pick me for your Minister and do it here in my over-grown garden? "

"Because of our parents." the Bride's voice turned suddenly sad.

"They were driving us crazy," the Groom admitted. "From the day we told them we were going to get married, they started to take over our lives."

"What made it even worse was that *his* parents couldn't agree with mine on any of the details. They kept arguing and fighting with each other over the cost of everything, trying to drag us into it. We just wanted to get *married*—who *cares* about the rest of it?" Tears welled in the Bride's eyes and trickled down her cheek. She dabbed at them with her veil.

"It got so bad that we started to fight between ourselves," the Groom said. "We even talked about forgetting the whole thing and calling off the wedding. He squeezed his new wife's hand and pulled her close against him.

"That's when we knew we were in trouble," the Bride agreed. "We realized that what was important to us was our love for each other. We didn't want to have a big wedding in the first place—it was my mom's idea…"

"*Both* our mom's ideas," the Groom added. "Only their ideas didn't agree."

"We wanted to get married for each other, not for them— and that's what we did!" The Bride kissed her groom on the tip of his nose.

"How much is your fee, sir?" The Best Man asked, digging into his pants pocket.

"Nothing. This one's on me," I said.

They all looked stunned.

In truth, I was stunned myself. The bride's dress alone cost as much as I made in two or three months of full-time work. Their parents had been prepared to spend as much for their kid's wedding as I made in an entire year of teaching community college. Probably more!

But money was not the primary reason I performed weddings. At that time my full-time teaching job paid me enough to live on and support my family. The ceremony we had just performed together was a sacred event, an intimate moment of shared truth and commitment between conscious human beings.

In this case it was also a subversive act!

How could I put a price on something so priceless?

"Look at it this way," I said. "You just saved a lot of money on a huge blow-out wedding that's not going to happen. You can use your savings for a down payment on a new home. I know you're going to have a wonderful life together because you already know what's right for you and you're willing to act courageously to do the right thing. You're obviously not going to be ruled by others or pushed around or bought off by your families. Congratulations! You really are husband and wife now, not just two kids defying your parents. You've been baptized by fire, and I'm proud of you. Two spirits so firmly united will never be defeated!"

They looked at each other in amazement, beaming like twin suns rising over a cloudy sea. I walked them around the side of my house and ushered them out through my broken garden gate.

As he opened the car door, the Best Man removed an envelope from his inside coat pocket and handed it to me. "Even if you won't name a fee, please accept this donation to your ministry," he insisted.

"Whatever's right," I agreed, sticking the envelope in my suit coat pocket. "I'm not here to argue, just to help."

Standing beside the Groom's black Mercedes parked at the curb, we all shook hands. Then the newlyweds climbed into the back and waved goodbye. The Best Man was going to drive them to San Francisco Airport, where they were flying to the Bahamas for their honeymoon. As soon as the plane took off, the Best Man would call both sets of parents and inform them of what had just occurred, explaining that the marriage license was signed and in the mail, so it was too late to change anything. The couple had already canceled their wedding reservation at a popular local resort, and had cancelled contracts with their caterer, DJ, florist, and other vendors scheduled for the event.

The newlyweds would have to deal with the family fallout when they returned, but I was confident they would overcome all adversity.

It felt so good, at least this once, to see Romeo and Juliet escape the trap and break free from the poison of feuding families.

Marriage Soup

My phone rang at 10 p.m. one Friday night during a break between rainstorms and winter floods. I had been reading stacks of student essays for hours and was grateful for any distraction. I was interested the moment I heard a woman's soft sweet voice asking if I was the Traveling Minister. She said her name was Kim and that a mutual friend had recommended me to perform her wedding ceremony. Was I interested?

"It's possible," I agreed. "But first I need to know where and when? Do you have your marriage license yet?"

"Yes, we got our license last week and our blood test results arrived in the mail today. The moon is high, we're tired of waiting. We'd like to hold a small ceremony tonight at our house up here in Bonny Doon if we can find some one who will marry us. Can you help?"

Although I was a single parent and rarely went out at night, it just happened that my pre-teen son was visiting his mom in the city for the weekend, so I had no pressing reason to remain at home. A late night excursion into the redwoods to perform a small private wedding sounded enticing. "Sure," I agreed. "Do you want me to wear my suit?"

There was a pause as she covered the mouthpiece of her phone; I could hear a muffled discussion in the background. She was laughing when she came back on: "Not unless it's a bathing suit. Doc says he wants to be married out on our deck, sitting inside our new hot tub. The whole wedding party will be in there with us, and of course you're invited to join us, if you like. You certainly won't need your tie. You won't need a suit, either, unless you mind being naked."

I paused to consider. This was California, 1978, where today was the first day of the rest of your life and "Go for It" was the theme of the decade. Some women were even giving birth underwater, so why not hold a hot tub wedding as well? Marriage *was* the ultimate immersion, after all.

"Sounds good to me," I agreed. "Should I bring my own towel?"

"No, we have plenty." She sighed with relief. "Thank *God!* You're the last name on my very short list! The last guy we called was *so rude*—he acted like it was an insult for us to even *ask* him at this hour of then night. But it's *early* for us!"

She gave me the address and instructions how to get there and in a few minutes I headed out the door.

The full moon was playing peek-a-boo through threatening storm clouds as I negotiated the tree-lined, curvy mountain roads up to their secluded mountain home. I found their mailbox on Pine Flat Road and turned in through their open gate, following a newly graveled road a short distance to their house. It was after eleven oclock when I pulled into their driveway and parked. The full moon loomed straight overhead, gleaming through a hole in the clouds and surrounded by a ragged patch of stars that glittered like crystal in the freshly washed sky.

It felt so good just to be alive! It was a great night for a wedding.

The recently built two-story house had lots of skylights,

large windows, redwood decks, and a bank of southward pointing solar panels lined along the roof. A nearby portable saw mill suggested that the builder had used wood from trees growing on his own land to build his house. Everything gleamed with newness, raw and fresh in the moonlight.

When I rang the doorbell a lovely, long-legged lady with flame-red hair greeted me at the door. She was wrapped in a deep blue Japanese kimono covered with pairs of white and gold flying cranes. "Hi. You must be the Minister. My name is Kim."

I recognized her voice from the phone. She smiled and shook my hand. Hers felt damp. "Come in, we are *so* glad that you're here!"

I followed her through their large, high ceiling living room into a tiled kitchen where we paused for a moment while she opened the refrigerator and removed two bottles of sparkling wine. "Doc asked me to bring these out for the toast. Would you prefer something non-alcoholic?"

"I'll drink whatever you're drinking. I've never tasted Korbel Sparkling Chardonnay."

"It's addicting," she assured me. "Do you need anything else?"

"No. I assume you want a stripped-down secular ceremony, right?"

She laughed. "Stripped-down is right. Nude is more like it. Doc and the others out back in the tub are all naked. Is that okay with you? Otherwise we could put on our bathing suits. That's about as formal as Doc is willing to get."

"Naked is perfect," I said. "The Birthday Suit tradition goes all the way back to the Garden of Eden, I believe. Besides, I'm a local boy. I've spent many wonderful hours soaking in the hot pools of Esalen, Tassajara, and Paraiso Hot Springs. For me, taking off my clothes isn't a problem, its finding hot water to jump into."

"Then you've come to the right place. Our tub has dozens of water jets to massage your shoulders and back and even your feet."

I followed her out onto their huge redwood deck where four people simmered in a bubbling cauldron of water. A thin luminous vapor hung over the pool, making it moon white and mysterious.

"Hey, Reverend, come on in. Add your flavor to the People Soup!" A long haired man called to me from the pool. He held up his hand and helped Kim into the pool as she slithered from her robe and slid in beside him.

I stripped off my clothes, and as I sat down on the edge of the hot tub, I said, *"This isn't a night, it's a wedding! Take off whatever veils remain!"* Then, holding my breath, I sank straight down to the bottom of the tub, immersing myself in the womb-warm liquid where all I could hear was the sound of water-jets and my own heart roaring in my ears.

I came up 20 seconds or so later and took a deep drink of the cool mountain air. "Delicious!" I pronounced. "What a great idea—a hot tub wedding! Thank you for thinking of it."

"You're welcome, Reverend," the long-haired man said. "That was a great line about taking off our veils. Did you write it?"

"No, it was written by a Sufi poet named Rumi, translated by another poet named Coleman Barks. That was just a poor paraphrase of the real poem, I'm afraid."

"I liked it. I've heard of that guy, Rumi. He started the Whirling Dervishes in Turkey or someplace like that, didn't he?" The longhaired man reached across the tub and shook my hand. "I'm Doc, Kim's about-to-be husband. This guy next to me hiding behind the beard is Allen, my Best Man. That's his wife, Ellen, next to him. Going on around the tub, the lovely lass to Ellen's left is Sheri, Kim's best friend from college. You've already met Kim, so this is it, the whole motley crew."

"Sheri's my Maid of Honor," Kim explained. She handed me a wine-glass and filled it with bubbly liquid, then filled everyone's glass. "I propose a toast!" She lifted her glass and we all lifted ours. "To The Traveling Minister, who came all the way out into the wilderness to marry us."

"I'll drink to that," I agreed. "But if this is wilderness, I can hardly wait to see real civilization!"

We clinked our glasses together in the middle of the tub and drank. The sparkling Chardonnay slipped down my throat like cool refreshing water. Almost instantly I felt the vapors rising to my brain. Or was it the heat from the bubbling water? Suddenly, the outside and the inside were the same; bubbles and steam, the stuff of our dreams. I grinned and sipped again.

"Got any more poems for the occasion, Reverend?" Doc asked.

"This whole occasion is a poem, my friend, and all of us are in the marriage soup together. But here's another love note from Rumi: *When I am with you, we stay up all night. When you're not here, I can't go to sleep. Praise God for these two insomnias—and the difference between them!*"

"I'll drink to that," Sheri said. Was it the moon on the glass, or did she wink at me? Oh Lord, I groaned silently. I've been alone too long!

"My turn for a toast," I called. We lifted our glasses. "To the marriage of Doc and Kim, which is happening right now as we speak! *Kim and Doc, please answer this key and crucial question: Do you take each other as husband and wife?*"

"We do," they said simultaneously. They glanced at each other, surprised.

"Question number two: Do you have rings?" I asked.

"We're already wearing them," Kim said. "They're a matched set." They held up their hands to show their slender gold bands. Kim's ring was nestled next to a slightly thinner diamond engagement ring that reflected half a dozen tiny sparkling moons.

"We put them on in the store yesterday to try them on," Doc said. "Then we couldn't get the damned things off."

"Your rings are *blessed* things, not damned," I corrected

him. "They're symbols of wholeness and they indicate your completion in each other. If you can't get them off, that's a sign you were meant to keep wearing them. So congratulations! Doc and Kim, you have pronounced yourselves husband and wife!"

"Isn't it supposed to be 'man and wife'?" Sherri wondered.

"No," I insisted. "Here at the end of the 20th century it has to be either man and woman or husband and wife. Separate but equal. If marriage transforms a woman into a wife, then it had better change a man into a husband or you've got trouble!"

"I'll drink to that," Ellen, the best man's wife, agreed. "To Doc and Kim, husband and wife; may you have a long and happy life!"

"She's a poet but she don't know it," the best man laughed. We clinked our glasses together and sipped again from the savory Chardonnay. Curls of steam kept rising from the tub, bathing us in warm mist.

Then Doc and Kim put their glasses down on the edge of the pool and kissed for a long time while we applauded, whistled, hooted, called for them to stop, begged them to stop, and finally splashed them until they finally did stop kissing.

When they finally came up for air, so to speak, Doc raised his hand, pointing one finger toward the moon. "I just have one question for you, Reverend—are we *really* married now? Is that all there is to it?"

"Yes. This is as easy as it gets," I said. "The only thing left to do is for me and at least one witness to sign your marriage license. I'll take it back down the hill with me when I leave and drop it off at the County building Monday morning."

"I'll be damned," Doc said. "If I'd known it would be that simple, we would have done this long ago."

"You've been *blessed*," I insisted. "Be careful what you think and say, especially on your wedding day. Every word sets a tone for your new direction. Change your expression and you'll change your life!"

"You mean if I start saying 'I'll be blessed' I will be?" Doc asked.

"Right on! Now hold that thought for the next fifty years." We laughed, and then Ellen, the Best Man's wife, jumped out of the tub and took a picture of us with our glasses lifted.

I climbed out when Ellen jumped back in so I could take a picture of their whole wedding party, bobbing up and down in their bubbling cauldron of people soup! This was certainly the wettest wedding I ever attended.

Since I was already out of the tub, I dried off quickly and dressed. It was chilly outside the hot water.

Kim went into their bedroom and brought out the paperwork so I could sign their marriage license. She handed me a check for my services while Allen and Sheri signed as witnesses. Allen opened two more bottles of sparkling Chardonnay.

As Sheri refilled our glasses, her eyes seemed to soften when she looked at me and I felt my heart climb up into my throat. The sizzling wine was flavorful indeed, as she handed me the glass, but I suddenly desired a little sip of Sheri!

That's when I knew it was time to leave. The first glass may have been ceremonial, but the second glass would be party and incline me in a direction I was not prepared to go.

"Goodnight, everyone," I said, setting down the trembling glass. "To quote a line from one of my favorite American poets, Robert Frost: *'I have promises to keep—and miles to go before I sleep'.*"

Waving farewell, I slipped back through their house and out the front door, their happy goodbyes still ringing in my ears as I drove back down the misty, moonlit mountain road toward my home.

Soul Mates

Somewhere there waits in this world of ours
For one lone soul, another lonely soul,
Each chasing each through all the weary hours
And meeting strangely at one sudden goal
Then blend they, like green leaves with golden flowers
Into one beautiful and perfect whole,
And life's long night is ended, and the way
Lies onward to eternal day.

by
Sir Edwin Arnold

Down through the ages marriage has taken many forms. The root of true union always entails recognition of our own soul's echo and desire. In the Western world this relation is called a soul mate. In the Eastern world, especially in China, this unique relation is beautifully expressed by the mystical concept of *Yuan* (pronounced yu-en)—the belief in a sort of predestination or fate that links true lovers together through time.

In both East and West, such love lasts long beyond the body. Many mystics assure us that soul mates seek each other out and keep connecting through time—which gives new meaning to the concept of "forever." The 14th century poet Dante Aleghieri expressed the essence of recognizing a soul mate in his poem, "Sudden Light."

"Sudden Light"

I have been here before
But when or how I cannot tell:
I know the grass beyond the door,
The sweet keen smell,
The sighing sound, the lights around the shore.

You have been mine before
How long ago I may not know:
But just when at that swallow's soar
Your neck turned so,
Some veil did fall—I knew it all of yore.

Has this been thus before?
And shall not thus time's eddying flight
Still with our lives our love restore
In death's despite
And day and night yield one delight once more?

Here, the subtle concept of continuance through time is clearly acknowledged through the poets longing for lasting love. Regardless of current scientific and logical rejection of such "psychic" theories, the concept of "soul mate" exists because the experience exists. Recognition that we have met our soul mate is a gut level feeling that is acknowledged by the other, this stranger with whom we suddenly have a spiritual connection. The act of "knowing" that this person is "the one" occurs beyond our more limited reason that demands physical evidence. For lovers who have ears to hear and eyes to see, the universe offers an infinite number of clearly visible clues.

Couples frequently confess that they "knew" the other was their intended at the first glance. This is a shared experience for far too many people for it to be called a mere coincidence. That it happens so often makes it easier for me to believe couples when they tell me, *"It was love at first sight."*

The Concept of *Yuan*

Here is one example of how the power of *Yuan* works to bring soul mates together. A few years ago James was a resident in medicine at Stanford University doing marathon 100 hour a week shifts. His social options were severely limited, but he wanted to expand his horizons beyond the hospital. He started surfing the net, hoping to make new friends. He was already using the internet to access a broad range of information, so he checked in on *Sinanet's* Club Yuan, an on-line Mandarin Chinese language dating service. That's how he met Teresa, who was the Marketing Communications Manager of *Sinanet*. They first exchanged messages in November of '97 and they "clicked" on many topics of exchange. They met for dinner on the day after Christmas and each of them knew, at first sight, that this was the one. However, they are both cautious people, so they started to date in a traditional fashion. It didn't take long for them to blend their lives together, in perfect balance.

To make the story even richer, it seems that James and Teresa's fathers had met through coincidence many years ago in Washington DC, where James' father was a diplomat from Taiwan and Theresa's father was working with a copyright delegation from Taiwan. Later, both families moved to California and settled in Silicon Valley. Then, twenty years later, their highly contemporary children, James and Teresa, met and fell in love in cyber-space. At their wedding, both of their fathers spoke of the mysterious unifying power of *Yuan* in bringing together their families.

Initial Recognition

The concept of a soul mate echoes through most of the world's great cultures. It emerges out of the human psyche when we "re-cognize" each other, even though we have never met in this life-time. To "cognize" is to know. To re-cognize is to know again. But how could we know each other "again" so deeply, so true, if we have not met before? In this vast universe, measured in trillions of light years of time, is it not possible that we *might* have connected in some past time and place?

Some mystics speak of whole families re-incarnating together through time. The clairvoyant Edgar Cayce even described whole cultures re-incarnating together. As an example, he cited ancient Atlantis being reborn in America, returning science and technology once more to its place of dominance.

Who can say how many cycles of time human civilization has gone through?

I only know that the depths of human love and compassion can never be measured. The belief that we have found a soul-mate is a living experience born in our hearts. The poet Kahlil Gibran defined that feeling perfectly when he wrote:

"You were born together, and together you shall be forevermore..."

More Soul-Mate meetings

In August of 1998, Jena was among the first five Chinese exchange students to come to study in this country in fifty years! On April 5th, 2001, Jena was introduced to Milton at a Chinese Dim Sum lunch held by her Los Gatos High School teacher, Bun, and his wife Alice. Jena was half an hour late, but Milton was glad that he waited. Their first glance said it all. They recognized each other. She saw herself in his eyes, and she knew at that moment that something magical was happening to her. She had seen the swan in him, even though at first he appeared to be an ugly duckling. Their attraction turned to friendship, and as their mutual respect grew it blossomed into a love so strong it was to live or die for!

On July 4th of 2001 Jena and Milton had dinner at the Shadowbrook restaurant, in Capitola, where he slipped his specially written and designed "Tasting Menu" in with the regular menu. The Tasting Menu was actually a proposal of marriage, complete with vows, but Jena was hungry and kept putting it aside to read the main menu. Finally Milton offered Jena a ring and asked her to read the "Tasting Menu." She did, and accepted his proposal. After dinner, for desert, they went down to the sand and spread a blanket on the beach. As fireworks and waves crashed around them, they knew they had each met the one in a Love Forever Land.

Tasting Menu for Friday, January 10, 2003
Starters: Thursday, April 5th, 2001
First Date—Dim Sum arrangement by Alice and Bun. Beautiful presentation, radiant with energy and a gorgeous smile. Took some time for her to arrive, but it was worth the wait.

One Look—Once our eyes met, we knew. A single look said it all.

Exchange of Faith—A compliment and a phone number, couldn't resist the temptation to call you. Once I had a taste, I couldn't wait for more.

Main Course: April 5th, 2001—January 10th, 2003
Auditions—Bandera's for dinner. Friendly conversation. No uncomfortable silences. "How many kids would you like to have? (April 14th, 2001)

First Kiss—After the movie. "I'm too tired to go home." (May 17th, 2001)

Fireworks Under the Stars—July 4th dinner at Shadowbrook. On the beach with a blanket, fireworks, and waves crashing.

Precious Moments—Buy, designing, and arranging my new home, one of the most memorable moments of my life. I'm glad you were there to share it all with me. (Friday, August 3rd, 2001 picked up the keys).

Days to Remember—Five days in Orlando (August 2001),

seven days in Hawaii (November 2001), Central Coast Pismo trip (December 2001), 7 day cruise to Alaska (August 2002), Fort Ross Abalone diving trip (October 2002), and Christmas in Las Vegas (December, 2002).

Dessert: January 10th, 2003—Eternity

For A Lifetime—To share the laughter of life, the joys of success, the emotions of challenges, the brilliance of experiences together. To become the very best of friends for the rest of our lives together.

Stages of Love—Attraction turns to friendship. Friendship grows to respect. Respect blossoms into love—a love so strong it would be to die for.

Circle of Love—A complete circle of life, which includes your and mine, our children, your family, my family, and our friends.

This tasting menu tonight is a complete course of my love and dedication to you that will last this evening and every other moment that we spend together.

Valentine's Day

Ariel and Diana met on a double date on February 14th of 2000, during their senior year at UC Davis. They were immediately intrigued by one another and exchanged phone numbers before the meal was over. They went out on their first date to a cultural dance performance in downtown Sacramento. Afterward, they ended up walking through the park of the State Capitol, holding hands and sharing in meaningful dialogue. Being completely in the moment, they forgot those around them and started doing some midnight yoga on the lawn. Through the natural flow of their ongoing dialogue late into that same night, they found themselves holding one another on the steps of the State Capitol building where Ariel confessed to Diana, "I feel like I'm sitting with my best friend, one I've known since childhood!" Diana shared similar feelings with him. As the semester continued, their love blossomed and they found themselves falling in love. Upon Ariel's graduation, he traveled to Israel to work abroad as a hike leader while Diana continued her undergraduate studies in Davis.

That summer proved to be a very painful test of their love. Only days after Ariel's departure the two longed to be reunited. That was when they realized how much they wanted to be continually present in each other's lives. The writer Rainer Maria Rilke captured these lovers new understanding of one another when he stated: *"For one human being to love another: that is perhaps the most difficult of all our tasks, the ultimate, the work for which all other work is but preparation."* During that difficult summer, Ariel and Diana fully realized that God had created each of them with the other in mind.

When Ariel returned from Israel, he moved immediately back to Davis and worked while Diana completed her degree. As a graduation present to themselves, the two of them threw on their backpacks and went traveling through Central America together. This was a wonderful time in both of their lives, which not only instilled a love for traveling but deepened their trust and mutual respect for one another.

Upon their return, Ariel was accepted into the program *Teach for America*, where he was assigned to teach 7th grade Social Studies in inner-city Baltimore. Together the two packed up their 1980 Volvo station wagon and headed out to the East Coast where they began their professional careers. Diana has recently obtained her nursing degree from Johns Hopkins University and Ariel has taught for the past two years, completed his program, and received a Master's in the Art of Teaching from Johns Hopkins as well.

Last year, when Diana's parents visited the two in Baltimore, Ariel asked Diana's father's permission to marry her, and he consented. A few months later, during the summertime, Ariel and Diana went backpacking with Ariel's family in the Eastern Sierras. Ariel's mom secretly had the engagement ring, and she gave it to Ariel one afternoon as he and Diana took off for a hike on their own. Minutes later, Ariel found an ideal spot on the top of a mountain overlooking a glacier lake where he proposed to Diana.

In between tears, Diana said yes, and they lightheartedly went back to camp to share the wonderful news!

Hook, Line & Sinker

Marilyn and Farid met at an island resort in Alaska called The Waterfall. Farid ran one of the boats that took guests fishing for salmon. Marilyn was a waitress at the resort, but she also wanted to fish. She went out once on another boat but had no luck. Then she went fishing with Farid and it was love at first salmon. Without knowing it, she had hooked a fish and a fisherman at the same time!

The next day after the trip, a flower appeared on the pillow of Marilyn's bed. Every day for the next several days there were more flowers. All of the rooms for the staff at the Waterfall were multiple occupancy and none of the doors were locked, so anyone on the island could be Marilyn's secret admirer. This went on for two weeks until Farid stepped forward one day and introduced himself as the culprit. Marilyn was impressed. The warmth from his heart heated hers.

From that day onward they spent many hours out in the wind on the water watching humpback whales and sharing their great love of nature. They learned that they are both good at the art of communication and compromise. In matters of faith, they know that respect is the key to understanding. They still love to fish, but decided to cast a wider net to catch their future as a family. Before the summer was over they were engaged, and a few months later they were married.

The Usher Prince

Kathy and Gerald met at the wedding of Gerald's sister, Lori. They noticed each other immediately. Gerald was elegantly dressed in a tux and tie. He might have been his sister's usher, but from her first glimpse of him he was Kathy's Prince! Gerald loved the way Kathy kept smiling at him, but he held back from speaking with her because she was with another guy. All evening long Kathy wanted Gerald to ask her to dance, but her room mate escort kept her soul mate at a distance. However, by the end of the evening they finally spoke briefly and exchanged phone numbers. They met again the next evening and started dating. Immediately they felt close, like two halves meeting to become one. They quickly realized that they wanted to continue their lives together as husband and wife. Within a year they were married.

Rivers Merging

Federico and Marianna met twenty-seven years ago at Sweet's Mill Music Camp in the Sierras. Sweet's Mill is a private mountain retreat with a large pond for swimming and plenty of places to pitch your tent beneath a tree. Below the old lodge was a huge outdoor stage that was perfect for village line dances and spontaneous world music shows that went on all night long. Federico had been playing Flamenco guitar for years in San Francisco and at the Renaissance Pleasure Faire. Around midnight at the Faire, the Flamencos would often take over one of the stages and play deep music until dawn.

The moment she heard Federico play his guitar, Marianna was caught by the spirit of Flamenco, that *Duende* bug that gets inside and never lets you go. They recognized each other as kindred spirits, but they were each in relationships they could not leave. However, Marianna was so inspired by Flamenco music that, on Federico's recommendation, she started studying Flamenco Dance in San Francisco with Rosa Montoya. Marianna was determined to dance to Federico's soulful music.

Federico and Marianna had many mutual friends through their bond of music and dance, so they stayed in touch. Over the years they developed trust, respect and admiration for each other. As close friends, on three different occasions Federico stayed in various dwellings at Marianna's home in Watsonville, California, where several separate families lived in community. Flamenco artists came to visit them from around the world!

Marianna fulfilled her first dream of dancing to Federico's music many years ago. Finally the day arrived when they could fulfill their mutual dream and continue their lives together as husband and wife. Their lives were like two rivers converging; together they became strong and powerful, capable of great passion and also soft stillness. Together they are in balance; together they are whole and are more than before.

Their wedding vows also reflected their sense of deep connection as soul mates:

Marianna: *Federico, by marrying you I acknowledge before the world the soul bond I feel for you...*

And I will continue to honor and love you and our relationship as I do now...

Because I know that to be true...

I thank the spirits for guiding me to my soul mate at last...

Federico my love, I will love, honor, respect, and enjoy you as your lawful wedded wife...for the rest of our lives...May I dance to your music eternally.

With this ring of gold and diamonds and rubies...all of which you outshine...

I take thee Federico to be my lawful wedded husband.

Federico: *Marianna, my beautiful love...*

By marrying you I acknowledge before the world...the soul bond I feel for you...

I will continue to honor and love you and our relationship as I do now...

Because I know it to be true...

I thank the spirits for guiding me to my mate of the soul at last...

Marianna my love, I will honor, respect and enjoy you as your lawful wedded husband...for the rest of our lives. May I make music for your dance eternally.

With this ring of gold and diamonds and emeralds, all of which you outshine...

I take thee, Marianna, as my lawful wedded wife.

Making Nice

You would think that weddings should be joyous events, but sometimes the relatives and guests bring uninvited hostilities with them. Imagine what Romeo and Juliet's wedding reception might have looked like!

As a non-denominational Minister, I am often called upon to perform inter-racial and inter-faith ceremonies, which Minister's of more orthodox churches often prefer not to do. So I was definitely interested in the challenge presented when Rebecca, a divorced Jewish woman with two girls, and Amir, a widowed Muslim man with one son, asked me to write a ceremony that would satisfy both of their families without offending anyone. Amir was a CEO in his own computer firm in Silicon Valley. Rebecca was an associate professor of Psychology at a Catholic University. Many of their co-workers would attend the ceremony, along with their relatives.

Rebecca's family was orthodox Jewish; her parents were from New York City. Her grandparents would be flying in from Tel Aviv, Israel, where they lived. Amir's family was orthodox Muslim from Hebron, in the Israeli occupied territory that Amir called Palestine. They would also be flying in for the ceremony, probably arriving on the same plane as Rebecca's grandparents.

Amir and Rebecca had been living together for over a year. Their love was solid and they knew what they wanted. Amir's brother was going to be the Best Man, with Rebecca's brother Jeff and Amir's business partner as his Groomsmen. Rebecca's aunt, sister, and nieces would be the Bride's Matron of Honor and Bridesmaids. Her daughters were going to be Flower Girls. Amir's four year old son would be Ring Bearer. At the end, they wanted to have an inclusion ceremony for their children.

Both of their immediate families approved completely of their marriage. The rest of their relatives, however, were dubious, at best—or flat out against it. I urged them not to invite those who were opposed to avoid possible conflicts.

My job would be to put their guests at ease and conduct a ceremony that walked a line of peace between both religions. I was to honor everyone as I uniquely united these two brave souls. I ached with admiration for the courageous couple. Amir and Rebecca were daring to trust, to reach out, and to construct for their children a house of love out of their dreams and bright hopes.

From the first day I agreed to work with them, I carefully followed the news from the Mid-east. A week before their wedding a riot broke out in Hebron between the Jewish settlers and the indigenous Muslims over the tombs of the Patriarchs. Both religions rightly claim Abraham as their founder, but instead of that historic fact uniting them like brothers, it just seems to make them madder at each other.

Well, Cane and Able were brothers, too!

The fighting was still unresolved on the eve of the wedding, and prospects for the day seemed grim.

However, in spite of my apprehensions, my gut level feeling about their ceremony said: *yes, absolutely! Go for it!*

Performing this wedding seemed like *exactly* the right thing to do.

It Started In a Garden

Their wedding site was a peaceful park in Saratoga called Hakone Japanese Gardens, where sculpted paths meander through Oriental flower gardens, leading strollers past antique Japanese Tea Houses, waterfalls, and a large Koi pond with one large arched Japanese footbridge over a tumbling stream. The soothing natural surroundings were beautiful and neutral, free of any political overtones. Down near the parking lot was a fairly large modern hall suitable for large ceremonies and receptions. With rivers of relatives and friends streaming into town from many directions, this was going to be a large crowd.

When I arrived half an hour early on the day of the wedding, the parking lot was already filled, yet the place was amazingly quiet. The serious crowd seemed more in the mood for a funeral than for a wedding. Even the faces of the children looked so serious that I wondered if I had come to the right place.

Then I saw Amir waving to me, the only smile in sight, and I moved quickly toward his light. He was glad I arrived early. My presence gave him moral support. My beard and mustache were neatly trimmed and I had worn my best dark suit and tie for the occasion. For an added touch, I drew a white silk scarf from my pocket and threw it across my shoulders, letting it hang down in front on both sides. That single piece of cloth is a universal symbol of clergy, and seemed to set everyone at ease. Suddenly many of the guests started to smile, and I could almost feel their relieved thoughts: *Ah! The wedding minister is here!*

Even so, as Amir and I walked through the crowd toward the wedding site, the air felt electric. It was a lovely Spring afternoon, but I kept looking up at the sky, expecting a storm of clouds about to clash.

Soon the guests assembled and the marriage party lined up to walk in and take positions for our entrance. I must have been frowning or showing my tension in some way because I felt a slight tug on my sleeve and looked down to see a plump, elderly lady smiling at me. She was dressed in an elegant purple evening gown, wearing an orchid corsage, and smoking a French cigarette. She smiled at me, and all three of her chins quivered as she nodded her head up and down in a reassuring way.

"You look a little nervous, Pastor. But don't worry, it's not so bad as it looks. This is a good thing that's happening here today and we all know it. Take my word for it, today everyone is making nice!" She winked and patted my arm.

I smiled at her and squeezed her hand. "Thanks. I needed that."

The Reluctant Ring Bearer

The DJ started *Pachelbelle's Canon in D* and the groom touched my shoulder. "Time to go..."

We headed up the aisle, followed by the Best Man and the Groomsmen, and took our positions at the chupa.

Next, the Bridesmaids and Maid of Honor entered single file. Everyone turned in their seats to watch three amazingly beautiful women, dressed in modest, full-length matching blue gowns, walk down the Astroturf aisle to join the men at the wedding chupa. They were followed by the Bride's sweet daughters, ages seven and nine, who were dressed in pink organza dresses and carried baskets of flowers. They strutted down the aisle happily throwing rose petals onto the ground and sometimes at each other.

But when the Ring Bearer stepped out, his eyes were large with fear. Amir's four year old son had agreed to the job in theory, and he certainly loved his tiny tuxedo and patent leather shoes, even though he couldn't roll in the dirt. But when it came to walking down that aisle alone, with the eyes of over one hundred strangers fixed on him, it was too much. He stopped mid-way, burst into tears, and threw the ring pillow on the ground.

Suddenly Amir was running down the aisle toward his son, while at the same time Rebecca and her father came running up the aisle from the other direction. They reached the boy at the same time and knelt down on either side of him, soothing and comforting him. Meanwhile, both the Bride and Groom's parents and grandparents also rushed into the aisle, with everyone completely forgetting themselves, the wedding procession, even the wedding itself, in their mutual concern for the child.

Since both families were already assembled in the center of the aisle, petting the boy and reassuring him, I waited a few moments for them to gather their wits. Amir retrieved the rings from the pillow. The Ring Bearer went to sit on his grandmother's lap, sucking on a lemon drop that one of his grandfathers had magically produced from behind the boy's ear, turning his tears into laughter.

Since I had the microphone, I took a deep breath and said, *"Adoni!...Bismilla! Ladies and gentlemen, what we are witnessing is exactly what this marriage is all about! Rebecca, Amir, and their families have just demonstrated their mutual, basic, most human concern—to protect and comfort their children. The only thing sweeter than their love for their children is Amir and Rebecca's love for each other. So please stand for the entrance of the Bride and Groom and we can proceed with the ceremony."*

The audience laughed and stood up as Amir and Rebecca came forward and stood beneath the chupa facing each other, hand in hand. Their faces were shining, and they waved at Amir's son, who waved back.

Within a few minutes they had married each other, joined their families, and continued their lives together as husband and wife. They were still dancing and celebrating when I left an hour later.

And everyone *was* making nice!

Cake Walk

Over the phone, the groom said they wanted to be married on the edge of the world in Big Sur. There would just be a few people. So I put on my new suit and dress shoes and dove fifty miles down the California coast to the Red Barn shopping center in Carmel. I was to meet them at four o'clock in front of a bakery where they were picking up their wedding cake. From there I would follow them down Highway One to their special marriage spot.

I arrived a few minutes early and parked in a lot across from the bakery. A few minutes later two cars pulled up. A short, slender, barefoot man wearing tan shorts and a red and yellow Hawaiian shirt jumped out of the passenger side of the first car and ran into the store while the driver, a young woman, kept the engine running.

I walked over and knocked on the window of the second car. A lovely young woman rolled down the window and smiled at me. "Hi, I'm a Traveling Minister. Would you be Yolanda and Angelo?"

"You got it right. Glad you're here, man." The dark-haired

man in a blue Hawaiian shirt behind the steering wheel grinned at me as he reached across the seat to shake my hand through the car window. "Angelo Amichi," he said. "This is Yolanda, my blushing bride."

To my surprise, she really was blushing! She shook my hand politely. She wore a colorful Hawaiian print muumuu decorated with palm trees and dancing girls in flower leis playing ukuleles.

"As soon as my cousin Tony comes out with the cake, we'll head south. The wedding site is just a few miles down the road," Angelo explained.

Just then Cousin Tony emerged from the bakery carrying a white cake box so large he could hardly see around the edges. I thought he might trip on the stairs, but he made it over to his car without incident. The driver, a slender young lady wearing a loose purple paisley shift and flip-flops got out and unlocked the trunk. She shifted a large picnic basket so Tony could fit in the cake, and then carefully closed the trunk lid.

"Let's roll," Tony said, giving Angelo two thumbs up. He opened the door on the driver's side as I hurried back to my car. A few minutes later our three car caravan cruised down the spectacular coast highway toward Big Sur. From the size of the cake, I imagined there must be thirty or forty people waiting for us, and I wondered where they found a cliff big enough to hold that many people. The coast road is narrow and tricky to navigate, without much space for parking along the side.

We were well past Point Conception before Angelo and Tony pulled off the road onto a wide space near the edge of a bluff. Ours were the only cars there, and I wondered where all the people were. The bluff was rough and uneven, plunging recklessly down a ravine fifty or sixty feet to the water below.

"Where are all the other people?" I asked them as we got out of our cars.

"We're it," Angelo laughed. "We're the whole rowdy crowd.

We brought Tony and his girl friend, Linda, along as our two witnesses. We need them to make it legal, right?"

"Right," I agreed. "Actually, you only need one witness, but two is always a better number when it comes to marriages. Where exactly do you want to hold your ceremony? This cliff seems kind of rough to me."

"Down on Paradise beach," Yolanda said. "It's our own special place we found on our first date."

"It's the most sacred place I know, more than any church," Angelo assured me. "It's the edge of the world. You'll love it."

"I'm sure I will, but I thought you meant we'd be standing on the edge of a cliff or on a beach. I'm not exactly prepared to climb down cliffs." For the first time he seemed to notice my dark wool suit and my slick soled leather shoes.

"I'm sorry, man. I hope this doesn't bum you out. I should have told you. It's not that hard a climb. But look, don't worry, If you mess up your suit I'll pay you extra to clean it," Angelo assured me.

I knew it wasn't a question of "if" I soiled the suit, just how badly. But I was over sixty miles from home and still hadn't completed my mission. I couldn't quit now! "Hey—life's an adventure. Your offer sounds fair. Let's go for it," I said.

I followed them down the steep sandstone slope. The rough path had been carved over time by the erosion of wind and water and the feet and hands of the countless human beings who had braved this descent before us. Suddenly my shoe slipped on a slick part of the path and my ankle twisted. I slammed into the cliff as I fell.

So much for the suit! I was face to face with the reality of being fifty years old and not in the best of shape.

The Bride and Groom were already down on the short narrow beach of sparkling white sand below. Above me, Cousin Tony and Linda were shuffling guitars and picnic baskets from their car to the head of the path. I stopped for a moment to catch my breath and regain my balance. I turned slowly, leaned back against the muddy cliff, and gazed out over the cove. Crystal clear turquoise water sparkled and swirled around the rocks in the shallow offshore shoals before plunging suddenly into enormous blue depths. Long lines of waves rolled past us to crash against rocks a few hundred feet further down the coast. It was all so beautiful I completely forgot my throbbing ankle for a moment.

"Are you okay, Pastor?" Angelo called up to me.

"I just slipped in my city shoes and turned my ankle. I'm okay," I assured him.

"Hey, barefoot is perfect," Angelo called back. "You can take them off, as far as I'm concerned. We're on the beach." He and Yolanda were picking up rocks and shells and pieces of driftwood and tossing them into a pile near the foot of the path.

I untied my shoes and stuffed my black cotton socks inside them. I tied the shoe laces together in a loop around my belt so I could keep at least one hand free for climbing. I was carrying my black leather portfolio that contained the two typed pages of their wedding ceremony and vows.

Turning back to the task at hand, I concentrated on inching down the remaining twenty feet of the path, mostly on my butt, nursing my foot all the way. Once on the beach, I found a sturdy driftwood cane, rolled up my pant legs, and hobbled over the warm sand to the water. I waded in, and sighed with relief as the ice cold salt water washed over my ankle. About fifty feet out in the cove, floating on top of a forest of kelp, two small otters rolled on their backs, watching us.

Angelo scrambled back up the path to help haul down their stuff. Between them, Tony and Angelo made at least two or three trips each, bringing down food, guitars, a table cloth, a set of dishes and silver for five, five crystal glasses, and a huge ice chest containing several bottles of sparkling wine. On his final trip down, Tony carried the wedding cake, still in its white cardboard box. His bare feet seemed to stick to the sand like suction cups as he casually carried the huge, heavy confection down the treacherous path. We all laughed at him because he looked like a walking cake box!

Meanwhile, the girls had laid out a path leading from the base of the cliff to the edge of the sea. It was outlined by stones, sea shells, strands of kelp, and pieces of driftwood. When they finished, Yolanda and Linda slipped around a huge boulder, carrying a suitcase. From a second suitcase on the guy's side of the boulder, Angelo removed a white linen dress suit, and a white shirt. He quickly changed into his wedding costume. Barefoot, without a tie, he looked formally rustic, handsomely wild.

A few minutes later, Yolanda appeared from around the boulder. Her delicate white lace wedding dress billowed around her in the brisk off shore wind that blew her long black hair across her face. Linda followed behind her, still wearing her paisley purple dress.

Angelo and Yolanda walked back to the base of the cliff and held hands, waiting for us. Tony and Linda took positions on either side of the path, almost in the water. I stood in the shifting, shallow water between them, facing the land. The legs of my suit were wet and the seat of my pants was soiled from sliding down the path. My suit coat sleeves were scuffed and both front and back was stained by reddish mud from the cliff. There was nothing left to worry about, and my ankle felt great in the cold water!

Tony and Linda played the wedding march on their guitars as Angelo and Yolanda walked from the foot of the cliff down the flotsam path to the sea. They paused before me, holding hands.

I opened my portfolio and read the welcoming words of their ceremony:

"Today as we dance on the edge of the world, we give thanks to Mother Earth, Grandmother Sea, and the four directions. We call upon the Great Spirit and all those present to witness this sacred event. From this moment onward, Angelo and Yolanda will continue their lives together as Husband and Wife. Angelo and Yolanda, you may speak your vows to each other now"

Speaking spontaneously from their hearts, first Angelo and then Yolanda declared their undying love and affection for each other. They exchanged rings and sealed their marriage with a kiss. Then Angelo suddenly swept Yolanda off of her feet. Carrying her in his arms, he quickly waded into the water and threw himself forward, dumping both of them, laughing and shrieking, into the sea.

When they came back out, Linda provided towels for drying off and they changed back into their Hawaiian clothes. Meanwhile, Tony and Linda unpacked the picnic baskets and spread the tablecloth on the sand. They laid out the plates and silverware, carefully placing a wine glass at each setting. They unpacked savory fried chicken, pasta, salad, cheese and crackers, smoked salmon, olives and so many other goodies I lost track of the details. Sitting cross legged in the sand, I immersed myself in the feast. We toasted the health, fortune and bliss of the newlyweds numerous times.

Finally they sliced their wedding cake, cutting ample portions for all of us. It was as delicious as it looked—a light chocolate cake with raspberry filling and butter cream frosting. We were stuffed, yet 90% of the cake remained untouched.

"Why did you get such a big cake?" I asked.

"For all of our relatives back in Hayward," Angelo said. "We'll have a big feast tomorrow in my uncle's back yard, assuming Tony can carry it back up the hill and get it home in one piece."

"No problem—it's a piece of cake," Tony laughed.

The sky turned red as the sun dropped to within a few inches of the horizon. My ankle felt almost whole again. Yolanda brought out the marriage license and I showed Tony and Linda where to sign, then dated and signed it myself. When we finished, Angelo handed me an envelope. Inside was the amount we had agreed upon for my services, plus a generous amount extra for cleaning my suit!

Looping my shoes back over my belt, we started back

up the cliff. Half way up, we heard a high pitched whistle from the water. We turned in time to watch a line of leaping dolphins cut across the mouth of the cove, working their way north toward Monterey Bay.

"That's a lucky sign," I called back to the wedding party. "It looks like your marriage has just been blessed by the sea itself."

On the drive back home to Santa Cruz, I couldn't help reflecting on what a curious blend of planning and coincidence this wedding had been. For sheer beauty and a relaxed, laid-back *aloha* style, this wedding certainly "took the cake."

Weaving Families

Last year more than a million couples filed for divorce in the United States. Over thirty percent of them had children. So it should come as no surprise to learn that nearly a third of all the new marriages recorded every year are actually divorced parents courageously trying once again to create something whole out of their broken families. Sometimes only one member of the new couple brings children to the marriage, but it often happens that both members of the couple have children who will become part of the new family unit.

Back in the bad old days, when divorced parents with children remarried, the children were rarely considered. Often they were not even present at the wedding, unless perhaps to serve as a flower girl or ring bearer. They came as part of the package and were expected to accept, if not love, the incoming step-parent. No doubt that sometimes happens, but it is not always the case. The only job harder than being a step-parent is being a step-child!

Children form the core of every family, the happy heartbeat of every home. They are conscious beings with their own purpose and their own will. If your children are in accord with your decision to remarry, and are willing to participate in your wedding ceremony, rejoice and include them. If they say "no" or decide to back out at the last minute, that's fine, too. Honor their wishes either way. They are often shy, reluctant to stand before a room full of strangers. The incoming step-parent(s) can give your gift(s) and make your pledge or vows to them later, in private. It's even a good idea to include them when selecting their gift for the occasion. Ask the children what they might want as a symbolic kind of ring substitute—such as an engraved bracelet or medallion, a necklace—even a Game Boy, or a special watch! Your gift and pledge will serve as an opening gesture of peace.

If the children are included during the ceremony, it should be toward the end, perhaps after your Officiant pronounces you Husband and Wife. After you kiss, your Officiant can introduce the second part of your ceremony by saying: *"Today Adam and Eve wish to include Eve's daughters in their marriage ceremony. (Name each child)… please step forward… In presenting of these gifts, Adam and your mother promise to honor, cherish, support, and protect you with all of their love."*

Over the years I have co-created hundreds of inclusion ceremonies for families. Following are a few examples to inspire you, including some sample vows made by step-parents.

Negotiating Deep Waters

Bill and Linda were scuba divers, and they chose to hold their ceremony at the Monterey Bay Plaza Hotel, not far from the Monterey Bay Aquarium. The hotel's lower deck is built on piers extending out over a shallow beach which the couple often used as their base when they went on their dives. At high tide, the water surges up beneath the deck, often submerging the beach and the hotel stairs leading down to it.

The wedding ceremony took place on the lower patio, where the invited guests sat in neatly arranged rows. The wedding party entered from above, walking down a flight of stairs. To honor her family tradition, Linda wore a tight fitting red silk Chinese wedding dress which covered her from neck to mid-calf, with matching red shoes. This was her second marriage and Linda had already done the traditional American wedding with white gown and veil the first time around. Now she was honoring her Asian heritage.

Bill was born on Kauai, and his bronze skin created a stunning contrast with his white tuxedo. He also wore a pleated red cummerbund, white spats & shoes and a white top hat.

All three of Linda's daughters, ranging between 6 and 11 years old, were identically dressed in red blouses and skirts, with matching red leather shoes and red bows tied in their hair.

After I pronounced Linda and Bill Husband and Wife and they sealed their marriage with a kiss, I said, *"Linda and Bill have asked to include Linda's daughters in today's ceremony. To begin, let me read these words of advice from Kahlil Gibran's The Prophet:*

"Your children are not your children;
They come through you but they are not of you.
You may give them your love but not your thoughts,
For they have their own thoughts.
You may house their bodies but not their souls,
For they dwell in the house of tomorrow, which you cannot visit,
not even in your dreams.
You may strive to be like them, but seek not to make them like you.
For Life goes not backward nor tarries with yesterday.
You are the bows from which your children as living arrows are sent forth!"

When I asked, *"May we have the gifts for your children,"* Bill removed three necklaces from his pocket and held them up for the girls to see.

I said, *"Alice, Sara and Rose, these necklaces are symbols of your family's unity. Your mother and Bill want to give you these gifts today to remind you of their love and to represent their hope and joy made visible through this marriage. In the placing of these necklaces, Bill and Linda pledge to you their continuing love and support, even as they surround you now with their arms of protection. Alice, Sara and Rose, do you promise to love, honor, and respect each other and your parents?"*

"We do!" All three girls spoke in unison, as if they had practiced.

Bill placed a necklace around each girl's neck. They were all smiling when I said, *"Congratulations! You have pronounced yourselves a family!"*

Later the girls showed me their gifts. Attached to each golden necklace was a small golden heart, engraved with their name. When opened, each heart revealed two tiny colored photographs, with Linda on one side and Bill on the other, dressed in their wedding attire, smiling out at their daughters forever.

Additional Inclusion Ceremony

On another occasion we articulated the union this way: *"Charmane, by joining your life with Michael, you also enfold his children within your loving embrace. Since its inception, marriage has always been a family creating event. Your wedding day is a time to celebrate and honor your interdependence on one another. Each one of us has something of value to contribute to our family, to our community, and to our world. It's not by accident or chance that we are drawn to each other. Each of us has something to teach; each has something to learn. Tyler and Jacob, Charmane would like to bestow these special gifts upon you."*

Charmane knelt down and said, *"As part of our wedding it was important to your Daddy and I to include you. Both of you are such a huge part of our lives, and we love you very much. But most importantly, I want you to know how much I love you. I promise I will always be here to love and comfort you. Whenever you need holding, my arms will always be open. If you ever have a bad day at school and need someone to talk to, I'll always be there to listen. You both mean the world to me, and I'll always be here to care and look after you for as long as I live."*

The two boys, ages nine and twelve, received small boxes that they opened immediately, pulling out and putting on their new Swatches. For the next five minutes, while the adults completed the rest of their wedding ceremony, Tyler and Jacob stood mesmerized, pushing buttons like mad as they set all of the electric functions on their new watches, ringing the bells and alarms and joyfully ignoring the adults who were, after all, merely kissing.

Caleb's vows

One young incoming stepfather put it this way to his wife's three year old son:

Caleb: Geno, I promise to hug you when you are sad...
Whether you've been good or bad, I promise I will always be your dad.
I promise to protect you from the monsters in the dark...
I promise to play with you on the floor and take you to the beach or the park.
You are a bright shining star, my son.
I promise to hold you up high whether you've lost or you've won.
You have given me a love I never could have imagined, and you have given me your mother as my wife.
As your dad and your friend I will love you all your life.
Let this ring that I give you represent our special bond as father and son...
As three hearts have now become one.

***

Remember—young children are often shy. Try not to get upset if they fuss or cry when you're speaking your words of love to them. The shorter your speech, the better it will be for them and for you. Your whole purpose here is to sweetly assure them of your love.

Vows for Two
To conclude, let me share an example where a couple spoke vows to each other's children.
Rob said: *I love you, Lisa, and I love your children, Brittany and Austin, as my very own.*
I vow to be a loving, tender, and nurturing parent...
always there for Brittany and Austin...
Not only providing their physical and emotional needs...but also being a good listener...a loving counselor, and a friend
Lisa said: *I love you, Rob, and I love your daughter, Cassy, as my very own.*
I vow to be a loving, tender, and nurturing parent...always there for Cassy...
Not only to provide for her physical and emotional needs...but also being a good listener...a loving counselor, and a friend.

I submit that words of respect and compassion, spoken at the right moment, can make or break a relationship. If you treat your children with respect, they will reciprocate in kind.

They *do* appreciate being considered and included in your wedding plans.

Forever After

We met on a flower lined patio outside their rented motel room, near the edge of the cliff where they wanted to hold the ceremony in two weeks. From where we sat, we could gaze across the Pacific toward Hawaii, where their dreams still carried them. The sun was only three or four inches from the choppy horizon, but young children still splashed and giggled in the nearby pool, creating an eerie counterpoint to our discussion.

Sue was a petite woman in her early fifties, slender, vigorous, with a sweet smile and a kind of radiance all around her. I would hesitate to call it a halo, but her magnetic field was definitely charged with energy that poured like healing balm upon her fiancé, who sat partially upright in a wheel chair. Bob, had been a large man, but now his flesh hung loosely from his body due to rapid weight loss. He was connected to an IV morphine drip that hung from a portable stand beside his wheel chair. His ice-blue eyes were wide with wonder, like a child's, and his heavily veined hand seemed weightless when I shook it.

"I suppose you're wondering why we want to get married," he croaked, wheezing as he spoke.

"Who *wouldn't* want to marry this beautiful woman?" I countered.

"The Doctors gave him three months to live," Sue offered.

"What do those buggers know about the mysteries of life and death?" Bob scoffed. "I don't care what the Doctor's say. I believe in mind over matter."

"Well, I guess that as long as you mind, then it matters," I offered. "But medical science *has* learned a few things about illness. What kind do you have?"

"Pancreatic cancer. They say that it spread all through my body and there's no use operating. So we've been trying alternate therapies—why not? My favorite one is laugh therapy—ridiculous, really. We watch comedies ever day and I laugh my butt off! I don't think it has cured me yet, but laughing is better than screaming, don't you think? If I've got to go, I at least want to go with a smile on my face."

"We met in London, and we've been together for four years," Sue offered, adjusting his tubing and monitoring the flow of fluid into his arm. "We kept talking about getting married, but things always came up and we kept putting it off. We wanted to move to Hawaii and hold our ceremony there. That's been our dream since the beginning. Finally, six months ago, both of our houses finally sold, we bought our plane tickets and we were ready to go…"

"That's when this bloody cancer hit me! Terrible timing, don't you think? It's hardly fair. I mean, if there *is* a God, you'd think He'd be a bit more cooperative about these things, don't you?"

"It's not my job to second guess God. As for what's fair, all I know is that taking a larger view often helps me understand my own problems. We have to look at our *whole* life, not just the parts we want to remember."

"Maybe you're right, but what the devil. None of it matters

now. The past is past, including me." He sighed, staring out toward the choppy white-capped waves for a moment. He turned back to me, fixing his pale blue eyes on my own. "We are *determined* that we are *not* going to be cheated out of our marriage," he said emphatically.

Sue patted Bob's hand, calming and soothing him. "Everything's all right, dear. Don't worry, we *will* be married soon. That's why the minister is here, remember."

He closed his eyes and relaxed slightly.

"If you have the license and one witness, we could perform the ceremony right here and now," I offered. I understood their urgency.

She shook her head. "We haven't had a chance to get one yet. We were hoping to go today, but Bob had a small relapse this morning, as you can see. We'd like to hold our ceremony on the Friday of next week at this same time of day, around sunset. That would give my two sons time to come down from Seattle, and a chance for Bob's daughter to fly out from London. Would you still be available for Friday after next?"

"Of course," I said. "I'd be honored." I glanced back and forth between their suddenly smiling faces. The doctors might have given him three months, but I suspected their estimate was more hopeful than honest. I wondered if *Bob* would still be available Friday after next!

We spent the next half hour constructing their ceremony, discussing where the guests would be seated on the patio, laughing quietly when I suggested they come in together with their Best Man and Maid of Honor pushing Bob's chair.

The next day I wrote up their ceremony and mailed it to them.

A few days later my wife came home from the hospital, where she works nights as a nurse. She described a sweet man with a British accent she had just taken care of; she was impressed by how his lovely wife had stayed beside his bed all night, holding his hand. When I asked if the man's name was Bob, my wife looked surprised and said it was.

That morning I went to the hospital to visit them. They were surprised and pleased to see me. I spent an hour with them discussing their situation. Sue told me they had gone down to the County Building the day after our first meeting and bought their marriage license.

I asked them if they wanted to expedite their marriage plans, and they both said "Yes," at once. We agreed to meet again later that afternoon and perform the ceremony right there in their hospital room.

Sue made a few phone calls to let the witness know, while I went home to print out a copy of their ceremony.

Only three other people were present in the room when I arrived that afternoon—the couple who owned the Motel where they stayed, and a nurse who kept ducking in and out of the room adjusting monitors, tucking blankets, and adjusting Bob's bed. Several bouquets of flowers adorned the bedside tables and Bob was wearing a clean white shirt with a bow tie, his blue eyes blazing with light. The edge of his hospital gown stuck out from beneath the edge of his sheet.

"I'll bet this is the first wedding you ever performed in a hospital," he teased.

"That's true," I agreed. "I'll bet this is a first for all of us. Not everyone gets married under such unusual circumstances."

"*Blast the* circumstances," Bob scoffed. "You know what irritates me most about this whole thing? These so called doctors have the gall to say I'm dying from *natural* causes. Natural! Cancer is an invader, isn't it? It's a bloody mutation! What's so *natural* about that?" He was glaring at the nurse, who quietly patted Bob on the shoulder and turned up his morphine pump a notch.

"I can't answer your questions, although they're good ones," I answered. "But being in love is natural, too," I said quietly. "Are you ready to get married now?"

"I am *long* overdue," Bob sighed. "I suppose I'm as ready as I'll ever be. I'm sorry we don't have our lovely flower *leis,* but who cares? What say, sweetums? Shall we do it?"

Sue took his hand and smiled. "Yes," she agreed. "Let's do it."

I cleared my throat, opened my black leather binder, and delivered the ceremony we had co-created. *"We have gathered today to witness and affirm the decision of Bob and Sue to continue their lives together as husband and wife. They have been through a lot during the past year, from their determination to sell everything and move to Hawaii to their struggles with Bob's disease. Truly, if you can make it through this, you can make it through anything and stay together for the rest of your lives. Today you are manifesting your deepest wish—to live together as husband and wife, and you have received your children's approval and blessings. You have declared your love and fidelity to each other, and today we all bare witness to the deep sweet singing of your hearts. As long as that true communion of love lasts, so will your marriage remain alive! May we have your rings for blessing?"*

The motel owner handed me their rings and I said, *"Your rings are symbolic of completion, a close reminder of the ever-present love you share. You may exchange them as you speak your vows. Bob, do you promise to love, honor and cherish Sue, to share your life openly with her, to honestly respect and tenderly care for her for the rest of your life?*

Bob said, *"You'd better bloody bet I do!"* He placed the ring on Sue's finger and kissed her on the cheek.

I handed Sue the other ring and asked, "Sue, *do you promise to love, honor and cherish Bob, to share your life openly with him, to honestly respect and tenderly care for him for the rest of your life?"*

"I do!" Sue smiled through her tears and placed the ring on Bob's finger.

I said, *"Bob and Sue, according to the laws of the State of California, you have declared yourselves husband and wife. Please seal your marriage with a kiss.*

As they kissed, tears were pouring down all of our faces— tears of happiness mixed with tears of understanding. The motel owner and his wife signed the license as witnesses.

"You guys really *did* it..." the nurse said with awe. "It's so wonderful..." she gulped back tears, "...and so...damn... *sad*..." she whispered as she ran out of the room, embarrassed to have uttered what the rest of us were feeling.

If the newlyweds heard, they gave no indication. The Bride sat sweetly on the bed beside her Groom, embracing him. Their eyes were closed tight against the harsh hospital lights.

We tiptoed out of the room, leaving them to their destiny.

Two days later my wife told me that Bob had checked out of the hospital.

When I called their motel, the owner informed me he had driven them to the airport where they boarded a plane bound for Hawaii.

The Wedding Kiss

Love springs eternal out of our human hearts, and the wedding kiss expresses it in action in a way we all can understand. From a shy peck to a passionate pucker, the wedding kiss is the climax of every marriage ceremony. Love's veil is lifted and the lovers are revealed in a moment of tenderness and vulnerability.

It's a moment as sweet as the icing on a cake!

Some kisses, like the marriages to come, are short and rushed. Others take hours, even lifetimes to complete. The wedding kiss fuses future and past, reflecting who we were and are and will become in one marvelous pucker of time.

There are bold, aggressive kisses and tender, nibbling sips; kisses formal and dry, ceremonial and rigid, hot and heavy, loose and long. Eye bumping, nose nibbling lips may hit or miss their mate's mouth at that scary moment. Is the bride nervous? Is the groom anxious? Are the Bride's eyes open or closed?

The quality of the wedding kiss reveals a tremendous amount about the lovers' innermost state of being. Of course, every move we make reveals who we are, but most of the time no one is paying attention. However, for that one special moment of our wedding kiss the spotlight is on us; everyone we have invited to come to the wedding is watching as our most intimate natures stand exposed.

The wedding kiss is a public moment of private intimacy.

The kiss reveals our naked truth, in spite of our fancy clothes. This is where girls become women; boys become men. The sleeping Princess awakes and Prince Charming will never again taste as sweet. This is the crown of all romances, the Grail of every quest. Unconsciously, it's what we've all been rooting for, the happy ending to love's eternal tale.

And yet that moment emerges so suddenly, creeps up unexpectedly every time. There were the invitations to send and the dress to buy, the tux to rent or buy, then all the anxiety about who would be late, when to start, who stands where, the rings, the vows, each half of the couple so nervous they can hardly think..*"Repeat after me..."* and they speak those magic words: "I *do!*" followed by: "I *now pronounce you husband and wife."*

And suddenly here it is in a flash, the part we forgot to rehearse, the invitation to a lifetime of intimacy: *"You may now kiss the bride..."*

Each member of the couple spontaneously greets the challenge in their own unique way. The wedding kiss expresses an instant of fusion that can never be recaptured.

They seal their marriage with a kiss...and the whole world sizzles!

Emotions erupt as the lovers unite. Grannies and moms burst into tears. Grandpas chuckle, knuckling the edges of their eyes with gnarled fingers. Dads grin and glance around the room, winking at each other in a knowing way. Teenagers squirm, embarrassed. Little kids giggle and jiggle up and down while all the relatives smile.

This is a speechless moment in which everything is said. Suddenly the shy bride grabs her guy by the ears and plants a big juicy smack on his lips! Their synapses snap. Two spirits spark and their invisible feelings spontaneously ignite. The lovers flow into and out of each other's eyes.

Or perhaps the nervous groom unexpectedly swoops his sweetie off her feet and runs off stage with her in his arms as she flings her Bridal bouquet into the crowd. Their car door slams. An engine roars off in the distance. The reception party goes on without them and a good time is had by all.

Look! Two separate lives have interlocked. Their separate threads are now stitched into a larger weave. Whole tribes of strangers suddenly are kin.

Each marriage is a one-of-a-kind event. Count yourself blessed when you find your name on the wedding invitation of one of your family or friends. And whatever happens, don't look away at the moment of the Wedding Kiss—it's the defining event of the day!

photo: Illuminations by Sandra

Part Two: Short & Sweet

Photo by
Paul Megison

"This is love - to fly upward toward the endless heavens."
Rumi

Every Wedding Tells a Story

Your wedding day is the crowning point of your courtship. It's a happy ending and a new beginning, all at the same time.

But how many of your wedding guests know your special love story?

You invited them to come all this way to witness and celebrate your wedding ceremony with you, so why not tell them a little bit about how you met and why you decided to get married at this particular place and time?

Were you childhood sweethearts? Was he a blind date? Did you meet at the office? Was it love at first sight?

Following are a few inspiring examples of personal love stories which couples shared with their family and friends on their wedding day. The structure and flow of the stories can serve as templates for you, should you choose to share the high points of your courtship.

How, when, and where did you meet? What interests and activities do you share in common? Which special qualities do you most admire in the other? When did you first know this person was "the one" for you?

Such personal touches can lift the hearts of everyone present and make your marriage ceremony unique.

Enjoy!

Falling in Love

Peter and Stephanie had been Skydiving long before they were introduced at the Byron Boogie, an annual skydiving event in Byron, California. But once they met, they fell in love at terminal velocity!

On the first night after their group dinner, Peter asked Stephanie to dance, but she told him she was cold and had a headache. She was heading back to her tent. To entice her to stay a bit longer, Peter quickly offered his warm fuzzy sweatshirt and a Motrin. How could she say no?

They talked long into the night, and each felt completely at home with the other.

The next morning, along with 100 other skydivers, they took the plunge. While they were in the Drop Zone, Stephanie saw Peter swimming toward her through the Church of the Sky. As he got close, he boldly gave her a passing kiss. At that moment something sparked in both of them. They each knew they had found "the one."

Over the next few weeks they developed trust and respect. At every jump they checked and inspected each other's gear to insure their mutual safety. They became the wind beneath each other's canopy as they shared the adventure and thrill of the sport.

A few months later they also shared the pain of Peter's bone shattering impact when his steering toggle snapped during a high speed turn and he crashed at 55 miles per hour into the sand. It took four transfusions of blood and months of healing for Peter to recover. Stephanie was by his side day and night. Life became very precious to them both. They started to make important decisions together and grew stronger as a couple. While Peter was recovering at a hospital in Monterey, he became reflective and thought about all the good things in his life. He realized that what made him feel lucky and happy and gave him the will to live was his love for Stephanie.

Later that year, on Stephanie's birthday, they were back in Byron with their skydiving friends on a warm clear night beneath bright stars. The group set up Tiki torches and pulled their lawn chairs into a circle to watch Stephanie open her presents. After she opened all the other presents, Peter stepped forward to present his gift. He was wearing the same sweatshirt he loaned her that first night to keep her warm. Peter presented her with a large jade and purple gear bag that had a present in every pocket. In one pocket she found a blue fuzzy ring box with a note inside that said, *"I owe you one engagement ring."* Beside it was a cute little drawing of a ring and a small metal harness ring from a parachute. Just to be sure she understood his intention, Peter got down on his knees and proposed to Stephanie in front of all their friends.

When she realized he was serious, her mouth fell open with astonishment and the word "yes" dropped out without a second thought.

The next day they did their first jump together as an engaged couple, diving into their relationship.

A short while later Peter presented her with an engagement

ring that belonged to his maternal Grandmother. Stephanie's wedding ring was engraved with a maple leaf and a star to represent their joining of Canada and the United States. Peter's ring was engraved with two figures holding hands, free falling through the sky of love.

Instant Recognition

Claude and Suzie had each just come out of truly abusive relationships and they were afraid to open up, afraid to trust. Claude had met Suzie's mother in church a few weeks earlier during a counseling session for his teen age daughter. One Saturday while Suzie and her mom were in a Home Depot store, buying fencing for Suzie's dog, Spirit, who kept escaping from her cage, Claude walked past them and said hello. Suzie's mom introduced him to Suzie. Their eyes met, and something inside said, "Yes!" They liked each other instantly. Before they parted they made a date for the next day after church to get to know each other better.

Sunday afternoon Claude and Suzie drove down to Tannehill Civil War State Park, near Birmingham, Alabama. All afternoon they strolled through the peaceful forest, enjoying each other's company as they explored the civil war cannon foundry and its surrounding buildings. Finally they sat next to each other on the hill behind one of the old slave cabins. The more they talked, the better they felt about each other. They could feel their protective shields melting away as they laughed together, sharing their past and their dreams.

As evening approached, they noticed something unusual.

All of the fireflies in the area had lined up in a straight row about twenty feet long in front of them. Hanging like a hedge about three feet off the ground, the bank of bugs blinked on and off, on and off, in perfect unison, like a string of Christmas Tree lights.

Suzie felt chills run down her spine.

All the hair on Claude's arms and the back of his neck stood up straight and cackled with electricity.

At that exact moment, they each knew, without a doubt, *"This is the one!"*

A few months later they reserved the old Tannehill Church and held their wedding right there in the park. And you can bet they made sure their minister told everyone why their location had such a special meaning to them!

Valentine's Day

Tracy and Jim met the day after Valentine's Day when two
of Jim's neighbors, Christine and Kevin, invited them over
for dinner on a blind date. The day before, on Valentine's
Day, Tracy and some friends had visited the San Francisco
Zoo where she had taken a fascinating "Sex Tour"...learning
about animal husbandry. Needless to say, all through the
dinner party they laughed as Tracy shared her observations
from the previous day.

After dinner, for desert, Jim and Tracy shared the last of
Christine and Kevin's wedding cake. The carrot cake, now
known as the "like water for chocolate cake", was made by
Christine's aunt, mixing all the ingredients with love. Kevin
and Christine had liked it so much that they decided to have
a six month celebration instead of waiting a whole year for
their anniversary.

And it worked! Jim and Tracy both agreed, it was love at
first bite!

However, they were both fairly cautious people. They
went on one more double dates with Kevin and Christine

before they started seeing each other on a regular basis. Jim introduced Tracy to the sports of windsurfing and mountain biking, and they soon developed mutual trust and respect. Over time their friendship deepened into love, and on Valentine's Day two years later Jim decided to surprise her.

They decided to have an "anti-commercial Valentine's Day" celebration at Jim's apartment and spend the evening together away from their usual crowd. They were going to spread a cloth on the floor of the front room for a picnic and have cracked crab and a bottle of wine. Tracy thought she would surprise Jim and arrived an hour early with a car full of helium filled balloons.

But it was Tracy who was surprised—Jim was already there, cooking the crab. He hugged her and about twenty five brightly colored balloons floated up to the ceiling in the front room, leaving them in a forest of dangling ribbons. She had no idea that she was helping to set the mood for Jim's even bigger surprise.

As they began desert, Jim asked Tracy to sit down on the couch. He sat down on the ottoman in front of her. Suddenly it became clear to Tracy what was going on and she started to giggle as Jim pulled out the ring box he had hidden behind a pillow.

In spite of her happy laughter, Jim got down on his knee and proposed. She said yes before he even offered the ring, and a few days later they started planning their wedding.

White Water

Katrina and Pat met five and a half years ago on the American River during a company team building exercise. The more adventurous employees went white-water-rafting. Although they had passed each other often at work, they were immediately attracted to each other when they arrived at the launch site. It was the first time Katrina had seen Pat without his glasses—he had left his glasses at home—and she was struck by his blue eyes. They sat next to each other on the raft, where they were literally flung into each other's arms a dozen times, and saved each other from falling overboard at nearly every turn. By the time they reached their landing bridge below the rapids, they didn't want to let go. But of course they did.

It was a week later when Pat rode to work on his 750 Honda Saber and pulled up in front of Katrina. She had always wanted to go for a ride on a motorcycle, and she asked him if he would take her for a ride sometime. That weekend they rode through the Santa Cruz Mountains to Capitola for lunch with Pat's motorcycle buddy, Dale.

For Katrina, it was love at first bike! Somewhere between their white water baptism and the thrill of the open road, their lives seemed to merge. With her arms wound tightly around Pat's chest, they fit like hand in glove. Over lunch that day, Dale complained that he was going to have to find a new riding partner, because he could see that Pat's carefree days were over.

Grinning at each other, Pat and Katrina agreed.

A few months later on Valentines Day in Las Vegas, Pat tricked Katrina when he gave her a box of chocolates and said, "Let's pick each other's pieces."

Katrina was disappointed when Pat picked the foil wrapped chocolate covered cherry—or so she thought! She hated chocolate cherries and wanted caramel instead. But she was a good sport and opened the foil anyhow. Inside the wrapping, she found a ring.

Of course she said yes.

I imagine she said a few others things too, but they didn't tell me that part!

Love's Dialogue

In their attempt to declare their loving intentions to each other and their wedding guests, one couple chose to share their stories with their guests by describing their experiences and feelings for each other. After they entered and I welcomed the guests, Kirsten and Chris took turns stepping up to the microphone to speak. Kirsten went first, reading clearly from her notes:

Kirsten: *During my last quarter in college at U.C. Santa Cruz, I toured around California for the Natural History Field Quarter. On one of our trips, I found myself in a muddy marshland surrounded by hundreds of croaking frogs. My dear friend Camas and I reached down and picked up two of the green little creatures and kissed them on the lips, wondering to ourselves if they would turn into our princes. They didn't, and so we imagined that our princes were waiting somewhere else for us in the world.*

"Several months later, I called Camas to excitedly tell her that I thought I had found My Prince. "His name is Chris," I told her. "He has a beautiful smile, big blue eyes and the greatest dog."

"How do you know he's the one?" Camas asked.

Well, I don't know for certain, but it sure feels right. Everything in my body tells me so."

I have spent the last three years and eight months discovering why Chris really is my prince—warts and all! When I am with Chris I feel balanced. He is self-confident, creative and humble. He treats people with respect, he loves and appreciates his family, and he is thoughtful and generous beyond measure. So what if he burns the toast sometimes and forgets to water the lawn?

Shortly after we were engaged a few weeks ago, my final doubt was put to rest when Chris received a late birthday gift from his friends, Danny and June. He opened up the small box and pulled out a Beanie Baby. It was a little green frog named "Smoochy," that reminded me of the real one I had kissed many moons ago, wishing for my Prince. Chris looked perplexed. He had never collected Beanie Babies before and didn't understand why they had sent him this gift. But I certainly did, and I knew it was much more than coincidence!

Chris, there is no doubt in my body or mind that you are truly my Prince. I knew I could let myself fall in love with you when I realized that you accepted me as I am, goatiness and all, and that I could open myself up to you and feel both vulnerable and safe at the same time. You bathe me in unconditional love, and it makes my heart melt and gives me a sense of hope because your love is so pure. You've taught me that loving someone and sharing my life with another person doesn't mean giving up my independence. I love and cherish who you are and what we are together. You make my life complete."

***

Her smile was radiant as she stepped back, yielding the microphone to Chris. He spoke as if narrating a dream...

CHRIS: *"We woke up early that morning. It was cool. Santo sprinted across the perfectly smooth dunes, leaving his tracks like so many lizards and beetles had done the night before. As we climbed the dunes the morning light curved across the sharp crests of sand, fell behind shadowy walls, and danced across ripples left by the wind. We climbed higher along the ridges of sand and so did the sun. The dessert began to warm. Rich red and brown bands ran across the faces* *of Last Chance Mountains as they became visible behind the pale dunes. When we arrived at the top of the dunes we sat there silently. The dessert stretched below us for miles. The White Mountains, covered with snow, were visible to the northeast. Dark volcanic domes surrounded the southern end of the valley.*

Then you turned to me and said, "Take off your clothes...No, really, don't look so surprised, it's fun!"

So I did...and we began to slide down the leeward side of the dunes. The dunes began to sing as the cascading grains of sand vibrated against each other. We played on the dunes, rolling and tumbling and running up and down until we tired. When we finally headed back, the sand was beginning to get hot. We found a cool shadowy bowl in the dunes. We rested our backs against the sand, sharing oranges, stories, and laughter.

And this is how it is when I am with you. I am surrounded by love and beauty. I have a friend to relax with as well as share new adventures. You show me things in myself and give me balance. I found someone special when I met you, Kirsten, and today I am happy to be sharing the rest of my life with you."

Shifting Gears

Craig and Julie met in 1991 at the Pixie Deli in Rio Del Mar. Craig was working as a convenience store manager at the Deli the day Julie stopped in for lunch. Julie was a die-hard motor-sports fan, and she couldn't help but notice that the entire store was decorated with all sorts of racing signs and favors supplied by various beer vendors. In fact, she had never seen any thing quite like the way this Deli had been decorated except for maybe at the Indy 500, but not in a convenience store.

Julie and Craig struck up a conversation, sharing in their excitement for racing of all sorts and vehicles. Unfortunately, Julie was already in a relationship, but Craig and Julie decided to remain friends, sharing their stories of road trips, back roads, camping and bench racing. They both shared a passion for speed and wanderlust and discovered that Craig had been in 49 states by the time he was 23 years old. Julie had been in 48 states by the time she was 25.

For a number of years Craig and Julie shared in adventures with their friends. There were motorcycle trips, camping trips, trips to the track, road trips and other adventures. The friendship deepened and flourished. When Craig would be off on a cross-country motorcycle trip, Julie would only have to send a psychic message for Craig to call, and within a matter of minutes her phone would ring. There was clearly a very deep connection.

When Julie would ask, "Why aren't you dating someone?" Craig would respond, "I am waiting for the right girl to be available." He always knew that she was the one for him, just as he knew that the man she was with did not love her.

Julie also knew that the man she was with did not love her, and after years of heartache she ended that relationship. Her friends, Joe, Glenda and David, offered Julie support and wise council through this very difficult time. So did Craig. Although it had been difficult and taken great strength, Craig had known better than to intervene. He felt strongly that if he had intervened any sooner, God would not truly bless their relationship, so he fought to stay positive. Although it was very difficult, Craig had the inner strength it took to wait for years. Now, at last he could tell Julie that he loved her and that she had always been the one for him. He softly held the sides of her face and told her all the things he had been longing for years to say. She was the only woman he had ever pictured as his bride.

Although Julie had often times thought Craig would make a wonderful partner, and she loved him deeply, she held this secret close to her heart all those years. The feeing of closeness to each other was always there, but never spoken, not even when they were gazing at a full moon while at a concert, or watching the sunset while sitting several feet apart. Craig had been the one who had cared for her, taken her to the hospital for surgeries and offered protection when her work required travel to unsavory places.

When Craig finally told Julie how much he loved her, she no longer had to wonder if she would ever be able to spend her life with her best friend. Neither Craig nor Julie could picture the future without the continuing, ever closer love and companionship of each other.

Many people have said Craig and Julie were the last ones to know they were in love and it took them forever to figure it out. That's okay; the timing was perfect for them.

Match Dot Com

Rachel and Erin met on Match Dot Com. Erin saw Rachel's profile and realized she was his perfect match. He immediately sent her an email, but she didn't respond because she had starting dating someone else. However, a year later, Erin revisited Match Dot Com and saw that Rachel had again posted her profile. He decided to give her a second chance. This time, Rachel responded to his email right away, and after a series of phone calls and emails, they went for a picnic at Shoreline Park in Mountain View.

Erin brought Brie and black forest ham on baguettes, and they sat on a bench overlooking the lake and talked for over an hour. They liked each other immediately, and dated regularly until Rachel went away for a two-week vacation with her family at the end of June.

When Rachel returned from vacation, Erin picked her up at the airport. He told her he was taking her right home because his parents were visiting and he had to get right back to them. Rachel wanted to spend time with Erin because they had been apart for a while. She thought that Erin seemed to be avoiding introducing her to his parents, so she insisted on going over to his house. Erin was shy about introducing Rachel to his parents so soon, but his parents and Rachel hit it off. In fact, Erin's mother convinced Rachel to come back over the next three days and help them paint Erin's condo! During that time, Erin's mother took Erin aside and said, "Erin, this girl is a keeper! She's in it for the long haul!"

Erin and Rachel continued to date, and over time their friendship deepened into love. They loved outdoor sports, and to celebrate the New Year, they went skiing at Mammoth Mountain. The cabin they were staying in was incredibly hot and Erin was so cranky from the heat that Rachel thought he wanted to break up with her! However, after two nights of roasting, they found the manager, turned down the heat, and both of them started having a good time. On their last day they, as they were taking out the trash, washing dishes and making sure they hadn't left anything behind, Erin came up behind Rachel, wrapped his arms around her waist, and whispered in her ear that he wanted to start the New Year off right. "Will you marry me?"

She caught her breath and her whole body shivered like a shock passed through it.

"You stinker," she said. "You *would* wait until the last minute. I thought you'd never ask!" She turned in his arms and kissed him.

"Hey, don't you want to see the ring," he asked when they came up for air.

"Okay," she laughed. "Rings are good, too, but kisses are better."

Soon they were looking for the perfect place to hold their marriage ceremony.

Overcoming Obstacles

Gary and Valerie worked in the same building for different computer companies. One day, Valerie gave a presentation at Gary's firm and Gary was impressed. He tried to talk with her, but Valerie was coming out of a hurtful relationship and her protective walls were strong. For several months they passed in the halls and Gary tried to get her attention, without winning even so much as a smile or "hello" in return.

Undaunted, one Monday morning he left his business card under her car's windshield wiper, inviting her to lunch.

Four days later she called him to say thanks for the lunch invitation, but declined, pleading "Not at this time." She told him her recent painful breakup and her fears. They talked a long time. Gary said he understood and told her the ball was in her court.

That was Friday. Gary thought about her constantly all weekend. But Valerie didn't call. On Monday Gary took back the ball and called her again. Valerie admitted she had been thinking about him, too. Gary immediately asked her out for an expresso during their lunch break. As they sat across from each other, sipping Café Mochas, they each felt completely calm and safe in the presence of the other. Their connection was immediate. They seemed to click on all levels—spiritual, mental, intellectual, and physical.

Being practical people, they continued dating and started to plan their life together. They decided to build their nest together and contracted to buy a house in the hills South of Silicon Valley on the bank of a creek. While they were inspecting the property, they noticed a pair of Gray Herons building their own nest in the Eucalyptus Tree behind the house. Gary and Valerie took that as a good sign.

They knew that in ancient China, Cranes symbolize family because they build their nest together, then move in and mate for life. It's an ancient, honorable, and natural way to proceed.

On the day of their wedding Gary and Valerie moved into their new house, and the last I heard they are still living happily ever after.

Heart Fires

Kathryn and Michelle met when they entered the San Jose Fire Academy's training class. They liked each other immediately and struck up a friendship. Over the next 13 weeks their job performance skills were tested individually, as was the relationship developing between them. The intense highs and lows of their training revealed their vulnerable sides as well as their strengths. They supported each other through it all, and one of the greatest gifts they shared was a common sense of humor, which has helped to carry their relationship to where it is today. On their one-year anniversary, Kathryn proposed to Michelle in their home. Michelle agreed not only to a lifelong partnership, but also to create a special ceremony to commemorate their partnership. They strive to be a part of the larger community and wanted to present themselves as a responsible loving couple. They have learned that others will respect you only if you respect yourself first.

When they declared themselves Life Partners, they exchanged these vows:

Kathryn: *I stand here today feeling truly grateful today and* *every day for having you enter my life. There have been some things I have questioned in life, but being with you has been the best thing that has ever happened to me. You have given me the sense of peace and belonging that comes from loving someone and having them love you back. You have given me the desire to look to the future and dream about all we have to experience together. I only hope I can give you a loving and fulfilling relationship for many years to come. As I give you this ring, I promise to love you for the rest of my life.*

Michelle: *This day is special because it allows me to stand before family and friends and express my devotion, gratitude and commitment to you. I dreamed of this day but lost the hope it existed. I had lost the hope of finding someone strong enough to be independent, yet vulnerable enough to allow another to love them. I have found that in you. You provide a safe haven for my fears and shortcomings, my hopes and desires, my emotions and passions. I have found a peace in my life that comes only when you have found a kindred spirit. From this day forward, I hold your heart in my care. I will nourish it with patience, kindness, and love. I will cherish my time with you as if this day were my last. I will honor your right to be an individual, but I offer my life to share. So in good faith, for the words I have spoken today, I give you this ring.*

Changing Oil

Ellen and Chris met just before Thanksgiving in November of 2000 at Bobby's Pit Stop when Ellen was working as a first grade teacher. She drove in and asked for an oil change, and when the manager said they couldn't fit her in, Chris stepped forward and offered to do it for her. A few days later Ellen stopped by again to thank Chris and asked him for his phone number. He gave it to her, but since he was nervous, he gave it to her backwards! So once again Ellen drove over to the auto shop. This time they made a date to have dinner at Al Dente Restaurant, where they closed the place down, dancing long into the night. They started dating steadily, going on walks, riding bicycles, visiting with friends and each other's families. They traveled around California and camped out. Over time their friendship deepened into love as they developed trust and mutual respect. During Christmas of 2002, Chris asked Ellen's father for her hand, and month later, on January 26th, Chris drove Ellen down to the most beautiful place in the world—Big Sur, California. They drove to the top of a Mountain ridge where Chris got down on one knee, offered her a ring, and said, "Ellen, I love you, and I'd like to spend the rest of my life with you."

Ellen didn't say yes right away—instead, she danced around in a circle screaming for joy! Finally she settled down, said yes, and Chris handed her the cell phone so she could call everyone she knew and tell them from the mountain top. By the time they drove back home, they had their wedding planned.

Fireworks

Since childhood, Sam always had a sincere passion for fireworks. Little did he know that it would be fireworks that would eventually cause him to find his true partner in love. In fact, it was Sam's fireworks and pyrotechnics website that first brought him and Lena together. One evening Lena was browsing the web from her home in China when she clicked on Pyrosamm's website. Lights! Action! Explosions! She was impressed, and sent him a message telling him so. They corresponded by email, and shortly thereafter, Lena invited Sam to an International Fireworks Festival in her home town, Liu Yang, China—the fireworks capital of the world!

Sam went to China for 10 days. He was fascinated, as he was able to visit factories and see how fireworks were made commercially. But he was even more fascinated by Lena. Although he returned home to the United States when the festival was over, he couldn't get Lena out of his mind. Two months later he returned to Liu Yang to stay with Lena and her family for the next six months. During this time he also worked with Lena for a fireworks manufacturer and exporter, where he learned about exporting fireworks. Then they traveled through China together as tourists, and their friendship quickly deepened into love. They decided to get married and applied for a Fiancé Visa for Lena. Sam returned to the States, and a month and a half later Lena followed him.

A few weeks after she arrived, Sam took Lena to a secluded private beach called Yellow Sand Beach, north of Santa Cruz, where Lena saw the ocean for the first time in her life. They had a picnic on the sand and a small fire on the beach. They had already picked out their rings and selected Shadowbrook as their wedding site, but Sam used the moment to propose to Lena a second time, more formally. When she said yes, Sam pulled out some Black Cat sky rockets and filled the night sky with exploding golden comets, crackling blue and red stars, and sizzling silver bees to celebrate their engagement.

There's nothing like starting out with a bang!

photo: Kurtz Photography

Part Three: Helpful Hints

photo: Kurtz Photography

"The fountains mingle with the river, and the rivers with the ocean.
The winds of heaven mix forever with a sweet emotion.
Nothing of this world is single. All things by a law divine.
In one spirit meet and mingle."
Percy Bysshe Shelley

Choosing Your Officiant

Your wedding day will be an intimate, highly memorable moment of your life. Your wedding Officiant will stand with you in front of your family and friends during one of your life's most special moments. Impressions from that person will be imprinted on you for as long as you live. He or she is also going to sign the legal document that will change your lives forever.

So choose carefully those people who will exert influence over your special day, especially your Officiant. Interview several Officiants until you find the person who resonates best with you.

Not all wedding Officiants are clergy. They can also be sitting or retired judges, ship and airline captains, town mayors, or justices of the peace. Many of them, including non-denominational ministers, can provide you with secular ceremonies that are not specifically religious, although they may still be spiritual. Of course, if you are getting married in your church, then your minister will provide you with the appropriate religious ceremony.

In many States you can even have a friend or member of your family sworn in for the day to legally perform your wedding ceremony and sign your marriage license!

Excluding churches, most wedding sites such as resorts, hotels, and restaurants have their own lists of preferred vendors, including wedding ministers, who they like to work with. If you plan to hold your ceremony in one of those locations, you would be wise to check out their recommendations first. You may also get names of Officiants from friends or family members. Other sources of reference are wedding web sites such as www.herecomestheguide.com You can easily find other web sites by typing in *Weddings* to run a search through *Google* or one of the other excellent search engines available through your personal web server.

It's a good idea to find an Officiant who lives fairly close to your wedding site, since many of us charge by the hour, including travel time.

The Interview

If possible, insist upon a face to face meeting with your Officiant so you can conduct an informed interview. To find a good match in your wedding minister, consider these questions: What kind of credentials do they have? Can they provide references from previous clients? Is their appearance acceptable? Do their voices project clearly enough for your guests to hear? Will they help you construct the ceremony and permit you to write your own vows? Can they conduct your rehearsal? Do they offer a contract stating their services and fees? Will they provide you with a copy of your ceremony?

In so far as possible, the person you choose to perform your marriage ceremony should reflect your own values, attitudes and beliefs. Unless you specifically request them to do so, wedding Officiant's are not required to lecture your guests or preach sermons or proselytize their faith at your wedding ceremony. He or she is your private employee, contracted to perform your marriage ritual, sign your marriage license, and go home.

Be sure you can trust them to stick to the script you agree upon.

Ask how they dress. Do they wear clerical robes or a special costume? (I prefer a neatly pressed three button dark suit.) Your Officiant's personal hygiene should be impeccable. Marriage ceremonies are usually up close and personal. Formal or not, they are often held under hot, stressful conditions where you and your Officiant will be in close proximity for ten—twenty minutes.

He or she should appear clean, neat, and appropriately dressed for your occasion.

If the Officiant passes all these tests and you both agree on the person, sign them up and rejoice! You're on your way to a wedding!

What to expect from an Officiant

Here is a short list of basic service that your professional Officiant should provide:

- Quick response to your initial contact via phone, e-mail, etc.
- A face to face meeting
- References & Credentials
- A written contract stating services and fees
- Co-creation of a written draft of your ceremony
- Able to conduct Wedding Rehearsal (when required)
- Prompt arrival at ceremony site in appropriate dress on your wedding day
- Performance of the ceremony as contracted
- Careful signing and timely delivery of all legal forms

Sample Wedding Contract:

Name of Officiant	Client's Name:
Address	Address:
Phone/Emai	Phone/Email:

Date and Time of Service:
Location of Service:
Rehearsal required:
Referred by:

My services as Wedding Officiant include:

*Sliding scale, from $A—$Z, depending on type of wedding & distance traveled

*Pre-nuptial meeting with you in person to generate material for the creation of your own unique wedding ceremony. Additional meeting upon request.

*E-mail, snail mail, fax and phone availability for quick communication.

*A first draft of your ceremony within 48 hours of receiving your deposit.

*Additional wedding related materials available upon request.(poetry, etc.)

*A printed final copy of your personalized wedding ceremony.

*Arrival at rehearsal and ceremony on time and in appropriate dress.

*A thoughtful and sincere presentation of your wedding vows.

*Signing your wedding license and overseeing the signing of your witness

*Filing of your marriage license in the county of issuance within 4 working days.

*References available on the web (web address if available) or upon request.

*Cell phone for easy access during travel on wedding/ rehearsal day.

*On-time delivery of service.

This contract acknowledges that I will write or help you to write your wedding ceremony, and perform your wedding/rehearsal service for you at the times and dates stated above.

A deposit of   was received by me on (date)_____.

The remainder of _____ is due on the day of the rehearsal, or after signing the official Marriage License.

Total fee for services: $Amount without rehearsal $Amount with rehearsal

Deposit   —Deposit   —Deposit

Amount due on date $Amount due $Amount due

Deposit: Check #

Signature of Client   **Date:**

Signature of Officiant: **Date:**

Groom's Do's & Don'ts

In the effort to organize a wedding, various members of the wedding party have roles to play. The Bride and her family have had a life-time to consider their roles and responsibilities—from writing out the invitations to paying for the wedding. Many books cover this information already.

But what's the Groom supposed to do?

Traditionally, the Groom is responsible for a number of things—from buying the marriage license, engagement and wedding rings, to arranging the wedding rehearsal dinner. Let's consider them in order.

All marriage license and other legal fees are paid for by the Groom, including paying your Officiant after he or she signs your marriage license. In addition to buying the wedding rings, the Groom is also expected to help pay for his Best Man and Groomsmen's tuxedoes and shoes. Gifts for the Groomsmen and Best Man are also the Groom's responsibility. The Groom provides boutonnières for himself and the entire wedding party, including boutonnières for the dads and grandfathers and corsages for all the mothers and grandmothers.

Of course, you'll need wedding gifts for all of your groomsmen and Best Man. If there's a Ring Bearer, include him too.

Some generous Grooms even buy the gifts for the Bride's party, from Maid of Honor and Bridesmaids to the Flower Girls.

Most important of all, don't forget to buy your Bride's flower bouquet and her wedding gift!

The Groom arranges and pays for the wedding rehearsal dinner. However, if the guys take him out for a bachelor party, that's at their expense!

The Groom gets to help select the wines, beverages, food and cake for the wedding reception, as well as hire (and pay for) the band. I urge Grooms to participate in as much of the planning as possible.

The Groom is also expected to help deal with any hotel or housing arrangements for guests coming from out of town. He's not expected to pay their hotel bills, just to help set them find lodging.

On the wedding day, the Groom must make sure all his attendants arrive at the wedding site on time, reasonably sober, and appropriately dressed. Your groomsmen may double as ushers, so don't' hesitate to ask them for help in setting up the site and seating the guests. Before the ceremony starts you should seat your grandmothers and your mom.

And don't forget the wedding rings! (Usually, the Best Man carries them and presents them when your Officiant calls for the rings.)

If you want a limo, it's up to the Groom to arrange for it—and pay for it, too. The Groom also pays for the honeymoon, but by then you'll be married and your bills will be shared!

The main thing is to set an affordable budget and stick with it.

In terms of disputed frill items, the rule of thumb is this: *Whoever wants it pays for it.*

A Dozen Duties for the Groom

1 Purchase your bride's engagement and both of your wedding rings.
2 Purchase the marriage license
3 Seat your grandmother(s) and your mother.
4 Pay for the limo and all transportation for bridal party.
5 Pay for tuxedo rental for Best Man & Groomsman
6 Purchase gifts for Best Man & Groomsmen
7 Purchase corsages for mothers & grandmothers
8 Purchase your Bride's bouquet of flowers, wedding rings, and wedding gift.
9 Show up on time with attendants for rehearsal and wedding ceremony!
10 Pay the Minister/Officiant's fee
11 Pay the Band and DJ
12 Pay for the Honeymoon

Marriage Knots

Couples who choose to hold their ceremonies outside in nature often seek non-traditional rituals to celebrate their unions. Two interesting ceremonies I performed will illustrate my point. The first relates to an ancient pagan marriage ritual. The second is part of the Nordic *Asatru* Religion.

Hand-Fasting

In the pagan tradition, no rings were exchanged. Pagans were usually peasants and poor. Therefore, their union was symbolic, rather than a display of wealth. The priest or priestess conducting the ceremony would ask the couple to present their hands, and then the Officiant would bind their wrists together in a figure eight, a "Celtic knot," or a simple bow.

This may have been the origin of the expression "tying the knot."

The Officiant should recite the following when conducting the ceremony:

These are the hands of your best friend, young and strong and full of love for you, that are holding yours on your

wedding day as you promise to love each other today, tomorrow and forever.
These are the hands that will work alongside yours as together you build your future.
These are the hands that will passionately love you and cherish you through the years, and with the slightest touch will comfort you like no other.
These are the hands that will hold you when fear or grief wracks your mind.
These are the hands that will countless times wipe the tears from your eyes, tears of sorrow and tears of joy.
These are the hands that will tenderly hold your children.
These are the hands that will help you to hold your family as one.
These are the hands that will give you strength when you need it.
And lastly, these are the hands that even when wrinkled and aged will still be reaching for yours, still giving you the same unspoken tenderness with just a touch.

Knife & Key

To honor the ancient *Asatru* religion of the Bride's father, one couple chose to include the tradition of exchanging a knife and key. The knife symbolizes the Husband's function as protector of his family. The key symbolizes the Wife's function as the heart and hearth of the home.

The Bride's father had specially engraved a fine carving knife that he gave to his daughter for presentation. The Groom had cast a large silver latchkey with a heart in the middle of it.

As the Bride presented the knife to the Groom, they both held onto it as she said:

I bring you this weapon
Wield it mightily and hold it well
In battle and in strength
As I stand by your side

The Groom placed his hands on the knife and responded,
I take this weapon well and wisely...
And I shall use it ever...

The Bride yielded the knife to the Groom.
The Groom then presented the key to his Bride. Once again they both held on to it while he said:
I give you this key to my house and my heart...
Hold it well and wisely, to be your strength...
As I stand by your side...

Reverently he released the key to his Bride, who responded,
I take this key well and wisely...
I shall use it ever...

***

Note, the *Asatru* ceremony should only be used by those people who practice that religion. The same sacred trust holds true for all religious. However, it does provide an inspirational model for couples to create their own exchange of symbolic gifts, with heartfelt words of joy and love.

Lessons from Ducks

These observations are based on the work of Milton Olson, a man who studied winged creatures for over 30 years, hoping he could learn something from them to use in our human lives. He began his studies when he discovered that ducks are never alone. In fact, they are with at least one other duck at all times and most usually in a group. Through his studies, Milton Olson gained insight into duck behaviors that provide lessons for all of us.

However, to reveal these insights during your wedding ceremony, you need help from your flock of supporters, who will form your left and right wings. This works best when you have a minimum of six groomsmen and six bridesmaids standing up with you. It will give everyone something meaningful to do

Perform Lessons from Ducks toward the middle of your wedding ceremony.

Members of the wedding party fan out on either side of the bride and groom like wings. Males form the left wing and read findings of fact. Females form the right wing and *interpret* the lessons to be drawn from each fact.

Remember that we need both wings to fly!

Starting at each wingtip, the lead groomsman reads Fact #1. The lead bridesmaid responds with Lesson #1. Each paired couple reads their Facts and Lessons, ending with the Bride & Groom who read Fact and Lesson #7.

Lessons from Ducks Readings

Fact #1: As each duck flaps its wings, it creates uplift for the birds that follow. By flying in a "V" formation, the whole flock adds 71% greater flying range than if each bird flew alone.

Lesson #1: *People who share a common direction and sense of community can get where they are going more quickly and easily, because they are traveling on the thrust of one another.*

Fact #2: When a duck falls out of formation, it suddenly feels the drag and resistance of flying alone. It quickly moves back into formation to take advantage of the lifting power of the bird immediately in front of it.

Lesson #2*: If we have as much sense as a duck, we stay in formation with those headed where we want to go. We are willing to accept each other's help and give our help to each other.*

Fact #3: When the lead duck tires, it rotates back into the formation and another duck flies to the point position.

Lesson #3: *It pays to take turns doing the hard tasks and sharing leadership so that no-one gets too tired.*

Fact #4: The ducks flying in formation quack to encourage those in front to keep up their speed.

Lesson #4: *In groups where there is encouragement the production is greater. The power of encouragement (to stand by one's heart and core values and encourage the heart and core of others) is what we need. We need to make sure our quacking is encouraging.*

Fact #5: When a duck gets sick, wounded, or shot down, two ducks drop out of formation and follow it down to help or protect it. They stay with it until it dies or is able to fly again. Then they launch out with another formation or catch up with the flock.

Lesson#5: *If we are as smart as ducks, we will stand by each other in difficult times as well as when we are strong.*

Fact #6: When ducks reach the physical maturation necessary to begin procreation, they search out a mate from among a neighboring flock to start a family. It is believed the differing genetics ensure greater survival.

Lesson #6: *A union should be strengthened not only by similarities and shared interests, but by differences as well. As with ducks, people are interdependent on each other's skills, capabilities, and unique arrangements of gifts, talents, and resources.*

Fact #7 Groom: Ducks mate for life. When one dies, the other never replaces his or her partner.

Lesson #7 Bride: *If we have as much wisdom as ducks, we will recognize our mate as our life long partner with the commitment and steadfastness of our winged mentors.*

Lovey Dovey

If your flock isn't large enough for the duck ceremony, it can be quite effective to perform a dove release at the end of your wedding. As the birds fly upward, they symbolize the couple's leap into a new life together. Like ducks, doves mate for life.

They also know where their home is and return to their nest at night.

Rose Ceremony

The Rose Ceremony is placed near the end of the ceremony before the Bride and Groom are pronounced husband and wife. Two roses are all that are necessary.

Officiant: *In the old language of flowers, a single red rose was considered a symbol of love and always meant "I love you". So for your first gift as husband and wife, you will give each other a single rose. Please offer and receive your first gift...*

Husband and wife exchange roses.

Officiant: *In some ways it seems like you have not done anything at all. Just a moment ago you were holding one small rose—and now you are holding one small rose. But in fact, you both have given and received one of the most valuable and precious gifts of life—one I hope you always remember—the gift of true and abiding love within the devotion of marriage.*

In every marriage there are times where it is difficult to find the right words. It is easiest to hurt and to be hurt by those whom we most love. It might be difficult some time to say the words "I am sorry" or "I forgive you"; "I need you" or "I am hurting". If this should happen, if you simply can not find these words, leave a rose at that spot which both of you have selected and let the rose speak for you. That rose says: "I still love you." The other should accept this rose for the words which can not be found, and remember the love and hope that you both share today.

Where ever you make your home in the future, please pick one very special location for roses, so that on each anniversary of this truly wonderful occasion you may each take a rose to that spot as a recommitment to your marriage based upon love. If there is one thing you remember of this marriage ceremony, let it be that it was love that brought you here today, it is only love which can make a glorious union, and it is by love that your marriage will endure.

Wine Ceremony

"Fill each other's cup, but drink not from one cup,"
Kahlil Gibran, ***The Prophet***

Every element of the wine ceremony is symbolic. Wine has symbolized both essence and blood for thousands of years in the West. In the Orient wine represents spirit.

For Christians taking Holy Communion, wine represents the blood of Christ. Christ's first miracle occurred at a wedding in Canaan where he turned water into wine for the thirsty guests.

The receptacle into which the wine is poured is also symbolic. The pouring of liquid from one container into another represents the transformation that is taking place.

Glass is transparent, fragile, revealing its content while shaping its form. Cups are tougher, often made of metal; they represent the larger life you will drink from together.

As the couple shares the wine, they are symbolically sharing their life. Drinking from one cup is also a way of demonstrating trust.

Some couples like to fill each other's cups and glasses.

Then they entwine arms and drink from each other's cup, which symbolizes your lives joining together. It also demonstrates how you must cooperate with each other under awkward circumstances, or the essence will be spilled.

Below is a non-denominational wine blessing a client gave me to use many years ago. I have adapted it for a variety of ceremonies:

***

Wine Sharing Ceremony:

Officiant: (Name of husband) *and* (Name of wife) *have chosen to sanctify their marriage through the following ritual:*

(Best Man or Officiant pours wine)

Into this cup (or these glasses) we pour fresh wine, which represents the human spirit. Over time the strong flavors of a new wine mellow and come into harmony with the wood of the cask. A new marriage also matures as a couple's strengths blend and are shaped by their experiences together. Now you two will share the cup of life.

(Officiant hands the cup to Groom and the Bride places her hands over the Groom's hands—or the couple lifts their glasses to each other.)

Many days will you eat and drink at the same table, sharing all that you have and all that you are. Drink now, and may the cup of your life be full to running over.

Husband and wife take turns sipping from the cup, or they can entwine arms and sip first from their own, then from each other's glass.

Drink it all down and empty that glass!

In the Jewish tradition, the empty wine glass is then wrapped in a cloth and placed on the ground. The Groom crushes it with his foot as the guests shout *"Mazeltov!"* or "Good Luck!"

The broken glass represents many things, primarily a breaking with the past. The Best Man usually gathers the pieces and disposes of them properly after the ceremony.

***

A Toast

In his poem, ***Rabbi Ben Ezra,*** Robert Browning said:

Grow old along with me, the best is yet to be,
The last of life for which the first was made.

The toasts come after the ceremony, and carry on through the reception. The best ones are uttered on the spot and come directly from your heart. Feel free to invent your own.

It's possible to create a wine or "essence" sharing ceremony of your own, to suit your taste and inclination. You can use any juice or liquid you like. Water, soda, champagne, liquor—they all serve the same purpose, but in my opinion they don't all share the same symbolic power as wine.

Candle Ceremonies

A Candle blessing

> *May the blessing of light*
> *Be with you always.*
> *And may the Sun shine*
> *Upon you and warm your heart*
> *Until it glows like a great fire*
> *So that others may feel the warmth*
> *of your love for one another*

To my knowledge, there is no one correct way to conduct a Unity candle service, nor is there a specific set of words anyone "must" say. However, the basic process seems to be fairly universal.

First, either the mothers of the Bride and Groom, or both sets of parents, step forward to light the first set of smaller candles. This can be at the beginning, middle, or end of the ceremony. These candles represent your family lines, burning since the dawn of time.

Because the ceremony is highly symbolic, it's not a good idea to try lighting candles outside unless they can be thoroughly shielded from the wind. You certainly don't want one or both flames to blow out before the final Unity candle lighting—nor do you want the Unity candle itself to blow out until after the ceremony is over. However, if one of the candles does blow out by accident, it's not a big deal. Remind the guests that it is the *intention* that matters most in this ritual, not the symbol itself.

Then relight the darn thing and get on with it!

Before each part of the ceremony, it's useful to have your Officiant or some member of your family say a few words to your guests regarding the meaning of each part of the candle lighting.

Following are some explanations from the past, a more contemporary rendering of these ideas, and an additional candle "kindling" ceremony.

Perhaps you'll be inspired to come up with words of your own.

Traditional

In the Jewish tradition, *The Baal Shem Tov* instructs us: *From every human being there rises a light that reaches straight to Heaven. When two souls are destined to find each other, their two streams of light flow together and a single brighter light goes forth from their united being. They do not lose their individuality, yet, in marriage, they are united in so close a bond that they become one.*

Following the profession of their marriage vows, the married couple then take up their smaller family candles and use them to light the large center candle. The two flames become one, symbolizing their new reality. In this way, they are saying that henceforth their light must shine together for each other, for their families, and for their community.

Contemporary

Officiant: (As Mothers/Parents light candles)

Now, we are going to engage in a ceremony of spiritual symbolism. The lighting of these first candles represents the Bride's and Groom's ancestral family lines, burning down through time to this point where they meet today. By lighting these candles, you each give light from yourselves so that your lives may join together as one—one in purpose, one in friendship, one in love.

Kindling ceremony

The Officiant begins the ceremony by saying:

Ancient sages say that for each of us there is a candle, a symbol of our own inner light, but no one can kindle his or her own candle. Each of us needs someone else to kindle it for us with a spark of love. When two people fall in love, they ignite each other's candles, creating great light and joy.

I'd like you to remember that moment in your relationship when you first realized you were truly in love and wanted to spend the rest of your lives together. Holding that thought, please approach the votive flame that symbolizes the eternal light of life in each of us.

(Groom's name) take this candle, symbol of your inner light. Light it from the eternal light, with the dedication to rekindle it again and again.

(Bride's name) take this candle, symbol of your inner light. Light it from the eternal light, with the dedication to rekindle it again and again.

With these candles, you can see how to achieve a beautiful marriage. Bring these lights, the symbols of yourselves, closer and closer to each other over the wick of the Unity candle, until they become one. (Bride and Groom jointly light a third candle).

This is the mystery of union, the fusion of two becoming one. The new flame dances, alive in the new life of your marriage.

Now your individual lives are illuminated by the same Source of love, with One Light, One Life, and One purpose.

Yet, it is vitally important to remember that there are always two people in a marriage, each with his or her personal desires, dreams and wishes. These must be respected with great compassion and genuine tenderness.

The spirit of your marriage must be lit and nurtured anew each day, even as we nurture our own bodies and spirits.

Remember—what burns must have substance!

May you burn brightly for one another throughout your life together!

Sample Vows

Your wedding vows are the heart of your ceremony, a defining moment in your relationship. The sacred words you speak to each other at this moment should reflect both your heart and your mind.

Many of us, overwhelmed by emotions, find it hard to express our true feelings in words—especially if we're going to speak them in public before our family and friends—the people we care most about in the world.

For members of religious organizations, standard or "traditional" vows are provided with the service. We need not worry about what we're going to say on our wedding day. Someone else will say it for us, and we just affirm, "I do."

For those of you holding secular or non-denominational ceremonies, crafting your vows can be a joyful challenge. It literally brings out the best in us.

Remember, it's not your specific vows that make your marriage legal—signing and filing your license and legal forms takes care of that. There are no rules for what you have to say or how you have to say it.

To me, that sounds like an opening, a place to create. Even one fresh promise made just for your mate can brighten up your vows.

I encourage couples to look at their many options. They can go with "tradition", or they can modify or use some one else's vows. They can also create their own vows, which I urge them to do.

However, we have entered the 21st century. It's time for a new kind of relationship between women and men. Therefore, I have removed the word "obey" from all vows. If you want it, you'll have to put it back in—and your partner had better ask why you want it! Instead, I suggest substituting the words "honor", "respect" or "cherish" in place of "obey."

Feel free to use any of the vows you see here. You can mix and match to create your own special blend.

Or better yet, let these examples inspire you to write your own!

My only advice is to keep your vows fairly short and to the point. If you plan to "repeat after me", it will double the time it takes to say them. If you want to speak your vows directly, I urge you to write them down on an index card for your Officiant to hand to you at the proper time. Even professional speakers use cards and prompts to aid them.

#1   Fresh & Contemporary:

a)   William, please repeat after me:
Alana, today I marry you…my best friend…
The one I laugh with… the one I dream with…
The one I love… You are the keeper of my heart.
I will stand by you forever…
With this ring I marry you…and pledge my faithful love.
(Place ring on Alana's finger)
(Alana's vows were the same)

b)   *Matt:* Katia, I promise to hug you when you are sad…

I promise to lift you on my shoulders when you can't see over the crowd...
I promise to shower you with kisses daily to keep your heart warm...
I promise to honor your decisions so that your soul stays free...
I promise to take care of our family so that we will feel secure...
I promise my eternal love...with this ring...I thee wed.
(Place ring on Katia's finger)
   c)   Gary: Jill...Just as there will never be a morning without the ocean's flow
So there will never be a day without my love for you
I promise to be your devoted husband...dependable as the tide;
As these waters nourish the earth and sustain life...
May my constant love nourish and sustain you.
With this ring I marry you...and pledge my faithful love

Jill: Gary *...may our love always be as constant and unchanging*
As these never-ending waves that pour beneath our feet
Flowing endlessly from the depths of the sea
I promise to be your devoted wife,
As bounded to you as the tide is to the moon.
With this ring I marry you...and pledge my faithful love

   d) *I take you, Barbara, as my wife...*
to share my love for the rest of my life,
and with all that I am, and all that I have...
to love, honor, and respect you...for as long as I shall live.

   e) Christina: *Ian, I take you to be my husband, my friend, my love;*
I will laugh with you and cry with you,
grow with you in mind and spirit,
listen to you and encourage you,
always be open and honest with you,
loving you without reservation,

for as long as we both shall live.
With this ring, I join my life to yours.
Wherever you go, I will go.
Whatever you face, I will face.
My heart and my home are within you.
f)   Connor's Vows to Elise:
We share a union of spirits,
a marriage of hearts, a love supreme.
This is a passionate moment in my life,
the moment I give myself to you as your husband.
Since you came into my life,
my days have been bright and glorious.
You and I are meant to dance to
the rhythm of life together.
Elise, I love you.
We are two bodies, but only one life.
May our days be passionate and long upon this earth.
With this ring I marry you, and pledge my faithful love.

Elise's Vows To Connor:
Connor, your impact on my life is immeasurable
You enable me to see the rainbows and laughter in life and
This makes me strive to a better person each and every day.
I love you Connor, and I love the treasures we have found in each
other.
I promise to be faithful and to unfailingly share and support
your hopes, dreams, and goals.
I vow to be there for you always.
Everything I am and everything I have is yours
from this moment forth, and for eternity.
With this ring I marry you, and pledge my faithful love.

g)   Alan: As I stand here today with the world as my witness,
I pledge to you my undying and everlasting love.
I will stand beside you as your partner
I will stand before you as your protector

And I will stand behind you as your solace.
Please spend and end your life with me.

#2   Blend of old & new

a)   Mick: *Beverly, I take you to be my lawfully wedded wife...*
To have and to hold in sickness and in health...
For richer for poorer...for better for worse...
Until death do we part...You are the keeper of my heart,
The one I live with...the one I trust...the one I love.
With this ring...I thee wed.
(**Beverly** repeats vows)

b)   Gary: *I take you, **Karen**, to be my partner and my*
friend...
To have and to hold you, forsaking all others...
To honor, respect and support you in good times and bad...
To be by your side in sickness and in health...
For richer for poorer... for better for worse...
I promise to love and to cherish you always...
For all the days of my life...With this ring, I thee wed...

c)   Henry: *I promise to give you the best of myself...*
And to ask of you no more than you can give...
I promise to respect you as your own person...
To realize that your interests, desires and needs...
Are no less important than my own...
I promise to share my time and attention with you...
And to bring joy, strength and imagination
To our relationship...
I promise to keep myself open to you...
To let you see through the window of my world...
Into my innermost secrets and dreams...
I promise to grow old along with you...
To be willing to face changes...
In order to keep our relationship alive...

I promise to love you in good times and bad...
With all that I have to give, and all that I feel inside...
In the only way I know how to love you...
Completely and forever...
With this ring...I thee wed...and pledge my faithful love.

d)   *Amanda/Greg*, *I give you this ring...*
as a symbol of my everlasting love for you...
Today, I give you my name and all that I am...
Please wear this ring as a symbol and a reminder...
Of my promise to love you, all the days of our lives...
I seal these vows with this ring
In the name of the Father and of the Son and of the Holy Spirit.

#3   More Traditional vows

a)   *I, Jon, take you, Marchelle, to be my Wife...*
To have and to hold...for better for worse...
For richer or poorer...in sickness and in health...
To love and to cherish...from this day forward...
With this ring...I thee wed...and pledge my lifelong love.

b)   *Laura*, *I take you to be my wedded Wife...*
To have and to hold from this day forward...
For better for worse, for richer for poorer...
In sickness and in health...to love and to cherish...
Till death do us part, according to God's holy ordinance...
And thereto I faithfully pledge my fidelity.
With this ring, I thee wed...
In the name of the father, the son, and the Holy Ghost. Amen.
(Laura repeats vows)

The possibilities for creating your own vows are limited only by our imaginations. Just remember, short and sweet is usually best—for you and for your guests.

The main thing is to be fearless.
Speak the truth of your heart and have fun!

Intimate Receptions

If you're single and looking for a safe, stimulating environment to meet a mate, try attending a wedding. Above all, stick around for the reception. From beginning to end, most weddings sizzle with intimate innuendo. Many ceremonies I perform are for couples who actually met at the wedding of a friend or a relative. Wedding receptions are fertile fields for finding future mates. Even the wedding of a stranger will do, providing you can get an invitation to the party!

At weddings, everyone is dressed in fine clothes, looking their best. Their faces shine with excitement. Emotions run close to the surface. People open up their hearts when they feel safe and protected, especially in the presence of close family and friends.

Therefore, it should be no surprise that while weddings sanctify and celebrate the union of two souls, the juicy receptions that follow often secrete more weddings. It frequently happens that people meet at weddings, fall in love, and get married within a year or two. If they were already dating, the wedding celebration serves as a catalyst, igniting in them the desire to join the merry married crowd. Before they know it, they are making out invitations for their own wedding feast.

Ceremonial Symbolism

Most wedding ceremonies are charged with subtle erotic symbolism. Why does everyone rise for the bride's entrance, but not for the groom's? Standing for the bride is clearly a symbolic response with sexual overtones. The flower bouquet itself evolved from blossoming stalks of wheat and grain to represent fertility. The bride's white dress symbolizes sexual purity. Her concealing veil is both a protection from the evil eye and a tease for the groom. Her veil hints at sweet secrets its removal will reveal; it evokes in the groom a fierce desire to see the face of his beloved.

In many ceremonies the father of the bride symbolically "gives" her to the groom for the purpose of creating a family. In the not-so-good old days, this was the moment when the father actually sold his daughter to her new master. In either case, a transfer of property, power, and responsibility is implied. Since the gesture is not legally required in California, many modern couples chose not to include it. It is also possible for both parents to walk in the bride. In the Jewish faith, both of the groom's parents walk in with the groom, as well.

Of course, it's also possible for the Bride and Groom to enter together, if they wish. If they have been living together, which is often the case these days, it may even be appropriate, since the Bride has already given herself away.

Entering together certainly symbolizes equality from the very start.

Even seemingly simple ceremonial acts, such as slipping the rings onto your fingers, the idealistic promises you make, and the kiss to seal your vows, are public gestures suggestive of deeper pleasures yet to come. The symbols quietly accumulate power throughout the ceremony until everyone's heart is surging. By the time your ceremony is over, something precious will have changed for everyone present. Through your marriage, they will now have each other in common.

Then the bride and groom shoot down the aisle like babies through a birth canal.

Their male and female attendants follow the newlyweds, linked arm in arm. Since they entered single file, their exit as couples mirrors the marriage itself.

A Time to Celebrate

Suddenly the pressure is off. Your ceremony is over. The Minister and witnesses have signed your marriage license and the deed is done.

It's time to celebrate!

The band strikes up a lively tune. Corks are popped and sparkling wine is poured for toasts. Ties are loosened, shoes fly off feet, hooks and buttons come undone. Through the alchemy of feasting and dancing together, strangers become friends and relatives become friendly. The atmosphere of a good wedding reception is open and relaxed.

For anyone romantically inclined, this is the time to be especially alert!

At the reception, the sexual symbolism becomes even more pronounced. The bride throws her bouquet to her bridesmaids, and the lucky lass who catches it will be the next bride—or so goes the myth. When the groom throws the bride's garter to his groomsmen, the lad to catch that intimate item of apparel is fated to wed within a year.

Does it work? You Bet!

So if you're single and want to change your status, that's all the more reason to get in line. If you're already married—duck!

Let's not forget the toasting, the sharing of food and wine, the cutting of the wedding cake. All of these sensual rituals are ripe with meaning. The final act of the wedding event, the *Honeymoon*, takes place off stage, in private. But that ultimate destination toward which all the festivities are directed never leaves the minds of guests or newlyweds alike!

The total effect of all these symbolic actions, charged with erotic and sensual energy, is to induce a living current of love into the wedding reception that leaps from heart to heart. Those who participate in the celebration get imprinted on each other. Sometimes, like the Bride and Groom, they stick to each other like magnets.

Soon they're looking for their own wedding Officiant!

The public witness of your wedding by family and friends puts a social seal of approval on your physical, sexual and spiritual bond. By blessing the newlyweds with gifts and pledges of support, the community reaches out to new couple in true communion. This assures us that love truly is alive and at work in the world.

A good wedding reception provides the perfect romantic atmosphere to meet your future mate or to re-spark your connection with your current spouse.

That's why wedding receptions often are the most intimate parties in town!

Thank you for celebrating with us

"Love is not two people gazing at each other,
but two people looking ahead together in the same direction."
Antoine St. Exupery
From Wind, Sand & Stars